Home Education
by Design

Published by
CrossHouse Publishing
PO Box 461592
Garland, Texas 75046-1592
Copyright Cynthia Lavoie 2007
All Rights Reserved
Printed in the United States of America
by Lightning Source, LaVergne, TN
Cover design by Dennis Davidson
Except where otherwise indicated, all Scripture taken from the
The Holy Bible, English Standard Version, copyright 2001
by Crossway Bibles, a division of Good News Publishers. Used by permission. All rights reserved.
ISBN 0-929292-49-9
Library of Congress Control Number 2007926966

TO ORDER ADDITIONAL COPIES FOR $12.95 EACH (ADD $3.00 SHIPPING FOR FIRST BOOK,
$.50 FOR EACH ADDITIONAL BOOK) CONTACT
CROSSHOUSE PUBLISHING
PO BOX 461592
GARLAND, TEXAS 75046-1592
www.crosshousepublishing.com
877-212-0933 (toll free)

This book is dedicated to my Lord Jesus Christ,
who covers over our vulnerabilities with His blood,
making all things new and all things possible,
for
"Unless the Lord builds the house, those who build it labor in vain. ..."
Psalm 127:1

Contents

ACKNOWLEDGEMENTS

*In the midst of a very busy life of home schooling, tutoring and just plain life stuff
it would have been very easy to just let this manuscript languish in my desk drawer, as it did for
some months over the past years. But because of the persistence of some beautiful women
in my life, the vision of my parents, and the tangible support of my husband,
not to mention the patience of my children, there is now a book to offer.*

*Therefore my heartfelt thanks go to Maggie Rayner, Wendy McNeely, Diane Down,
and Karen Effa who continued to ask various renditions of, "How is the book going, Cyndy?"
helping me to believe that this material was something worthy of passing on.
Without your encouragement, prodding, editing, and prayers I doubt I would have seen
this through to completion. Blessings.*

*And to my children: Alexis, Justin, Zachary, Danielle, and Rebecca, my home-based live test cases
for all the principles and fancy ideas presented here, thanks for keeping my feet on the ground with
your beautiful comments of "You're writing a book? I'm hungry, Mom!" I love you all.*

*For my parents, Art and Lyla Jean, who purposed to give me an "author's" name at birth,
thanks for your vision and your amazing support through the years. Blessings to the both of you.*

*To Michael, my love, for all the hours you "covered my back"
as I took the time to write, rearrange, write and rearrange some more
the contents of what you now hold in your hands, thank you.
Your tangible investment of time and resources in the midst of many hours strengthened me
and nourished my resolve to finish what has truly become a mutual project. I bless you.*

Introduction

It has been my observation over the years that there is very rarely one curriculum which is superior to any other—what one family swears by for math another detests; where one family loves a language arts program, another has found it impractical or cumbersome. So what allows a given curriculum to hit the mark for one family and not another?

I propose that rather than content or composition being the core issue of whether a particular curriculum will work for a family, it is more often a cocktail of time and season, the number of children and their ages, mom's teaching style, family lifestyle—these and more are the factors underlying the success quotient of matching a family with its curriculum. When tackling the chore of assessing curriculum, the answers to what, when, where, why and how to study have far more to do with your particular family, its chronological composition, and the make-up of the individuals than the brand, popularity, supplier or cost of the material in question.

During our fourteen years home educating I've spent a small fortune on curriculum that looked like "just the ticket" to sanity and success. The substantial array of books lining our living room shelves is really a testament to my book addiction completely legitimized by home schooling! There did finally come a point where I realized, "Oh my! Enough is enough." A number of years ago we had many more books than we were using at any given time, so I began looking for ways to utilize the books already on my shelf.

What came out of that search was a plan, a recipe if you will, into which all of the individual family ingredients could be cast into a pot and simmered. The result? A self-tailored unit of study for a family and its individuals. This is where this book will take you, but first we will spend considerable time exploring the unique dynamics of your family and how that influences the choices before you as you educate your children.

The decisions about what, when, where, why, and how to study can be quite overwhelming, especially for moms new to the game. I have found that just as I figure out the answer to each question, our family changes and I must ask new questions and search for new answers. Changing dynamics can be as simple as everyone aging a year and consequently changing grades, to moving, new babies, learning disabilities, terminal illnesses, and so on. However, once the initial questions of values and goals were answered for me, changing dynamics were less threatening to my sanity.

One of my goals in writing this book is to embrace with you your family's uniqueness. Just as God created each individual to bestow an essence of him, our families also become matchless in their composition, each of our family units has a flavor all its own, and it is this flavor or aroma that provides opportunity to be celebrated as we educate our children. Understanding, accepting, and embracing the reality of who we are during the different seasons of life facilitates wise educational choices. My hope is that this book will facilitate you doing just that.

Chapter One
A Vision for Home Schooling

The memories of my own decision to home school are still fresh. I'd been on a full track heading towards public schooling, and within a matter of days a number of my paradigms were flipped around. I was left feeling quite stunned to say the least.

I was waiting at my daughter's gymnastics class and I overheard another mom say, "I can't decide what schooling option to choose, public school, private school or home schooling." I was taken aback, for I was pretty sure this woman was not a Christian, and I had assumed that the only people who home schooled were Christians walking in fear of the world. But she had put all of the options together as viable alternatives. This really caused me to do some thinking. "Maybe, just maybe, home schooling was in fact a viable educational alternative."

That very night my husband brought home a book about how parents can broaden their roles as teacher with their children. "Hmmmm, interesting," I hadn't really thought about parents taking on a more formal teaching role before. And the very next day "Focus on the Family" had a program about home schooling. And for the first time I began to realize that home schooling just might be something worth considering. And so, within days we realized that this was indeed what we felt God was asking us to do. Although for just as many days I was in shock. Yet, I have been very grateful for God "calling" us to home schooling.

Regardless of whether you feel "called" or not there is obviously something that intrigued you or led you to consider home schooling. What is it that you've seen or heard about home schooling that has drawn you?

Why did I begin home schooling?
What was it that caught my attention?
What was it about home schooling that grabbed at my heart?
Why am I continuing to home school?

These questions must be carefully considered, for our answers speak of what we value. To value some thing is to apply to it worth. We may say a certain action is worthwhile, or that a certain person is worthy of respect. We describe an unwanted interaction as being worthless. In these sorts of statements we reveal what we value.

What aspects of home schooling have worth for you?

_____

_____

_____

_____

_____

I'd like to introduce you to three home school moms in my acquaintance. They graciously allowed me to interview them and convey their values and goals. I don't ask you to agree with these women. However, you can certainly see how their strongly felt values have forged distinct paths for their educational goals.

Maggie

Maggie is a mom in her forties with two school-aged teens, a boy, age sixteen, and a girl, age thirteen. Maggie values character first and foremost. The ability to get along with people of all sorts is a top priority for herself and her children. Maggie also values the desire and ability to seek learning independently. Coupled with this is the ability to think independently and creatively; to identify within oneself creative solutions to life's difficulties that no one else may have come up with. Maggie's values translated into prioritized goals look like this:

Goal #1

"My highest priority is to instill godly character into my children."
"I want to pass on to my children a passion for loving the Lord and others."

Goal #2

"Critical thinking is important to me, that ability to think outside the box."
"I want to equip my children that they may be competent to do whatever in life they choose to do."
"I want to give my children the freedom to not be constrained by traditional learning."

Goal #3

"I want my children to have access to a standard of education broader and more in-depth than what public school can offer them."
"I want my children to be academic in that they have learned how to learn."
"I want my children to have the skills to teach themselves."
"I want my children to outgrow the need to have a teacher."

Maggie remembers a quote she once read, "Outgrowing the need to have another teach is real success." This quote encompasses much of the whys and wherefores of Maggie's home schooling.

Jocelyn

Jocelyn is a mom in her early thirties with three children, a girl eight years of age, another girl who is five, and a boy of three. Jocelyn describes her goals.

Goal #1

"I want to grow world Christ followers."
"I want my children to be unafraid to offer Christ to the world."

Goal #2

"Genuine compassion and empathy is a gift I'd like to give my children."
"I want my children to be courageous to confront suffering with compassion."

Goal #3

"I see the equipping of my children that they may lead the next generation as part of my task."

These goals come directly out of what Jocelyn and her husband value. And it is their lives which reveal their values for they have just finished a year in the Philippines as missionaries and are presently discerning where God would have them go next.

Pam

Pam is in her forties and the mother of one school-age son of fifteen. Pam values strength and independence. Her desire for her son is to be able to walk strong in what he believes, to walk the walk for Jesus Christ, and to not be persuaded by the crowd.

Goal #1

"The most important thing to me is that my son is a follower of Jesus Christ."
"I desire that my son chooses not to conform but to always be questioning."

Goal #2

"I want the freedom to choose my own course outlines, which will encourage the love of learning, rather than being held to rigid learning outcomes defined by someone who doesn't know my son."
"I endeavor to provide my son with a mastery of skills that he may be equipped to seek answers to questions."

Goal #3

"I want my son to be strong, and to have a character that does not fall prey to the pressures of others."
"I want my son to have a great sense of self."

Pam desires that her son will be a leader who not only questions but has tools to seek answers to those questions.

As you can see each of these women has goals unique to who they are and what they value. Now it's your turn. Answering the following questions will help to define what you value and from there we will turn those values into goals.

Why did I begin home schooling?

_____

_____

_____

_____

_____

_____

What was it that caught my attention or grabbed at my heart? What books or quotes did I read, who did I talk to, that gave me a vision for home schooling?

_____

_____

_____

_____

Why am I continuing to home school?

_____

_____

_____

When someone asks me why I home school, what do I say?

_____

_____

_____

_____

As I contemplated this again for myself I at first found our goals difficult to define after twelve years of home schooling. Our values and goals have been knocked around by the reality of "us" through the years. In many ways they seemed lost under a pile of dirty laundry or a mound of dishes somewhere. Yet as I rethought through this I've been surprised and pleased to find that our foundational values have in fact remained; they seem to have stood the test of time continuing to do their job even when we were not aware of it.

Value 1: I desire to give our children the ability to know and live from their hearts, offering back to God what He has instilled in them as His gift to the world.
Goal:
- *"I will give my children opportunity to know their strengths and limitations, to be self-aware and passionate about what they have to offer to God and to the world."*

Value 2: A love of learning coupled with a freedom to learn as they learn best.
Goals:
- *"I will foster a love of learning by retaining flexibility in our educational choices."*
- *"I will allow them to learn according to their own style and at their own pace with material of our own choosing."*

Value 3: We desire our children to have the ability to be leaders for Christ with a Christian world view.

Goals:

- *"I will present to our children a Christian world view through a variety of resources, such as living books, coupled with dialogue appropriate to their ages as they mature."*
- *"I will model authenticity and integrity as integral elements of a leader's role, and will expose them to real life stories of those who have walked a path of leadership in the name of Christ."*

Value 4: That our children would be out-of-the-box thinkers.

Goal:

- *"I will train my children to ask questions more than being concerned with necessarily knowing the 'right' answer."*

When your goals are measurable, it is also much easier to filter anything coming into your home. Does this help me meet our goals? Does this thwart the purpose of my stated goals? It is a great exercise for spouses to work through their own individual values and goals initially, then as a couple make opportunity to formulate your unified values and goals for your children.

Summarize your own values and goals.

Value Statement 1:

_____

_____

Goals:

_____

_____

_____

Value Statement 2:

_____

Goals:

_____

_____

_____

Value Statement 3:

_____

_____

_____

Goals:

_____

_____

_____

Values reflect the core beliefs of who we are, and they may or may not change as we grow with the passing of time. Home schooling must serve our value system at any given time or it needs to be discarded, much as any endeavor we seek to undertake. Unless home schooling is serving us and what we believe we will become slaves to it.

It has been my observation that those who feel enslaved to home schooling do not remain home schooling for long. It takes so much energy to home school that to enter into it without believing in some intrinsic worth of home schooling leaves one without a vision to lean on during the tough times. Many families plan to home school for a year, reassessing each year as it comes along. Whether you are committing yourself for one semester, one year, or for years to come, knowing your values and goals will be girders around which everything else finds strength and purpose. So keep working this till you feel comfortable with it. It is well worth the time and effort.

Chapter Two
Home Schooling Methods

Now that our goals and values are clearly identified, it will be helpful to examine a few of the many different home schooling methods. Some folks have chosen one method to the exclusion of the rest. Others take bits and pieces from them all, using those parts that suit their family best. Sometimes different methods can be used simultaneously for different children within the same family, or different styles are used at different times depending on the needs of the children.

As you read the following short, point-form synopsis of different educating methods, keep in mind that there is no right or wrong way to home school. Enjoy the freedom to pick and choose what is best for your family at any given time. This is why you are home schooling! As you read through the following, it may be helpful to highlight the parts which really stand out to you. Thankfully, there are as many ways to home school as there are family styles and situations.

Unschooling
"Ultimate Flexibility"
- Doing it differently than schools
- Taking advantage of life's natural educational possibilities
- Using a child's natural curiosity to motivate education
- Goals are often learning to relax, enjoy time together with space to grow and mature
- Does not mean NO textbooks and no instruction

Wholehearted Education
"Learning to Live and Living to Learn"
- Based on a discipleship relationship between parent and child
- Follows 5 D's
    1. Discipleship Studies—God's word
    2. Discipline Studies—basics: math and language
    3. Discussion Studies—living books and fine arts
    4. Discovery Studies—nature, science, arts, creativity
    5. Discretionary Studies—life skill and abilities, natural gifts and community involvement

Independent Learning
"Emergent Learning"
- Believing that academic growth and learning is an individual activity
- Motivation through excellence
- Requires high standards
- Parents provide:
    1. High quality educational material

2. Good study environment
3. Excellent study habits (disciplined)
4. High academic standards

Computerized Education—Online Schooling
"The Way of the Future"
- Credit for college more easily acquired through this method
- Often uses government curriculum, but not exclusive

Unit Studies
"Integrated Subjects"
- Each subject integrated with and enhanced by other subjects
- Children immersed in topics from many angles
- Uses multilevel instruction as much as possible
- Balances textbooks with novels and other hands-on activities

Classical Education
"Learning to Think"
- Teaching children HOW to think
- Rigorous style of education using logic, Latin, Greek, classical history, and literature composition
- Effective in producing thinkers and leaders
- Style of "private tutoring" done by parents
- Follows the three stages of intellectual development: grammar, logic, and rhetoric

Charlotte Mason
"Living the Educational Life with our Children"
- Classic good books enliven imagination and are filled with good vocabulary and human emotion
- Teaching a child to recognize and admire that which is righteous, pure, heroic, beautiful, truthful, and loyal
- Uses narration—"telling it back"
- The child's mind does sorting, sequencing, selecting, connecting, rejecting, and classifying
- Early years are for developing the habit of emotion

Principle Approach
"Research, Reasoning, Relating, and Recording"
- Christian character and scholarship is the central focus
- Objective is to think biblically and to establish a firm Christian world view
- Focuses on seven principles:
    1. Christian character
    2. Biblical stewardship
    3. Sowing and reaping
    4. God's sovereignty

5. Covenant
6. Christian individuality
7. Christian self-government

Accelerated Education
"Intensive, Structured, Focused"
- Not forced education
- Rather, 12 months a year schooling
- Very structured and focused
- Motivation is by responsibility

Textbook/Workbook
"Planning the Work, Working the Plan"
- Intended to be highly structured
- Curriculum provider offers varied amounts of teaching assistance, marking and record keeping as requested by the parent
- Examples of complete curriculum providers: Christian Liberty Academy, A Beka, Bob Jones University Press, Sonlight, Tree of Life
- Examples of workbook suppliers: Alpha Omega, A.C.E., Christian Light Education

List the statements that struck you as particularly appealing. Think not so much about what sounded like it would be the right answer or a good idea, but about the statements which spoke to your heart, those that resonated with your now stated values and goals.

_____

_____

_____

_____

List the different home schooling methods you have used in the past.

_____

_____

_____

Which methods did you enjoy most and why?

_____

_____

_____

_____

Which methods did your children enjoy most and why?

_____

_____

_____

Now look at the first list you wrote reflecting what grabbed at your heart. Then look again at the methods you've been using up till now. Are there any differences? Are you home schooling in a way which supports your value and goals? If there are any discrepancies, my guess would be that you are finding yourself frazzled and frustrated much of the time, trying to school in a way that does not support what you value most. If this is the case, I suggest you make a list of changes you can make to get yourself and your children on track and in line with your heart's desires regarding education and how that plays out in everyday life.

You may have just realized that the method you've been employing doesn't at all line up with your values. Perhaps what you read here reaffirmed what you believed all along. Maybe you realized that by tweaking your methods your children might be served better. Whatever your situation, reflecting here may seal it in your heart.

Previous method used	Evaluation (in light of your values & goals)	Changes to make

The work you have done here will be challenged as you read the chapters to come. Yet it is good to have a place from which to start. It is good to know what our values are and how to implement choices that support those values. The equation that you've just begun to work on we will continue to add to in the following chapters. Hang on, it's quite a ride!

Chapter Three
Choices and Limitations

One of the ideals regarding home schooling I at one time adopted was the idea that home schooling would offer my children wider opportunities of choice as they went off into the world. While this may be partially true, I now realize that in reality there are far more limitations to my and their choices than I want to admit.

By its very definition the word "choice" imposes limitation. For when one choice is made another is automatically not chosen. Let me say this again, for it is critical that we get this. For every choice made there is an equally viable option not chosen.

When my son spends time learning to play an instrument, there is automatically something else which is not receiving that investment of time. If my daughter needs to work extra hard learning how to write well, the energy and time spent on that is withdrawn from other tasks and opportunities. Since there are only so many hours in any given day, we must therefore pick and choose carefully where we invest our time.

If we were not inextricably bound by time then choice would be irrelevant; it would merely represent a deferment of options until a later date. But we are in fact bound by time, and the time spent educating our children is brief and fleeting—no matter how far it seems to stretch into the future at the outset of the primary grades. Therefore, inherent in choosing is limitation. And these limitations we must become reconciled to, if not, there is a danger of carrying a discontent regarding all that is not being done, instead of a confidence in going forth, pleased with what we are doing.

Negative Space

Think of home schooling like painting a picture. A competent artist painting a scene pays just as much attention to negative space as to positive space. Let me briefly explain what these two terms mean and how we might apply them to choice. Positive space describes the space taken up by what is drawn while negative space is the empty space between and around what has been drawn. I think of the positive spaces as the choices we make while the negative space can be thought of as the limitations made by our choices.

Listen to what Mona Brookes, from her book *Drawing for Older Children & Teens*, has to say about negative space in regards to the art world:

> The confusion comes in, however, when we are told that we have to pay attention to the negative space when we are drawing. The idea of paying attention to nothingness is very foreign to most people. But when you draw, if you pay as much attention to the shapes and sizes of the empty spaces as you do the shapes and sizes of the objects you draw, you will master the best method available to capture proportion and scale.

If we use Mona's words as if she were discussing home education rather than art, it might sound like this:

> The anxiety comes in however, when we are told that we have to reconcile ourselves to what we are not doing when we home school. The idea

of paying attention to what we are not doing is very foreign to most people. But when home schooling, if you are reconciled to the ramifications and effects of the resulting limitations of your choices while focusing on the opportunities and outcomes of what you are doing, you will discover the best method available to capture balance and harmony.

I don't know about you, but I long for balance and harmony. Consider this in the physical world. When I designed and decorated my living room I paid careful attention to the balance of the room. And the balance of a room is as much dependent on what is not there as what is. I have been tempted from time to time to hang some family photos above our arm chair. Yet I know doing so would throw off the balance of the room and I'd end up dissatisfied, rearranging other areas of the room in hopes of achieving balance once more.

A room that is balanced is restful and soothing; it is a place that invites. So a life, when balanced, is restful to the one living it as well as to those who encounter it.

As with balance, harmony is created as much by what is not there as by what is there. We have wood furniture stained in varying yet complementary tones. The furniture is in harmony because each piece is complementary to the other pieces, but it is also in harmony because I've not placed furniture of unnatural finishes. So again, harmony is achieved not only by what we do, but just as much by what is not done.

Harmony and Balance

In order to create balance and harmony in our homes let's consider our own families as a blank canvas. We dab in a child here and there, a spouse, add a stroke for ourselves, the in-laws, the employer, meanwhile paying attention to the negative spaces as well as the positive spaces. Besides creating harmony and balance for the family as a whole, it is important to create balance and harmony in the lives of each individual.

In my living room I seek to create balance not only for the room as a whole, but also in each corner and on each wall. In this way the harmony and balance of each part adds to and enhances the balance and harmony of the whole room. If I did not pursue balance and harmony in any part of the room, the whole would cease to be balanced. So it is with our families, the choices we make and the ensuing limitations are to be reconciled with each individual as well as the family unit in mind. In this way the balance and harmony of each child's particular education enhances and in fact makes possible the harmony of the family unit.

As we home school we are bombarded by choice. Gone are the days when finding a decent math or science program was like looking for water in a desert. In today's barrage of choices it is far too easy to lose sight of who we are, who our children are and what our home schooling ought to be about. To further complicate this choosing from the many options available is the reality that in many cases we are no longer choosing between good and bad but between better and best. And this leaves us a dilemma of much greater proportion, for the criteria by which we choose is much more subtle and often elusive. How do we make good choices? What is a good choice? Could my "good" choice made for one child still be considered a "good" choice for another?

The dilemma of choice comes to us in a number of ways:

• What to and what not to study

• What angle we are coming from as we study

• What lessons we want to impart, which ones do we not

• What curriculum or method will we be using

For every math program chosen there are another dozen that were not chosen. Why? We need to be able to answer for ourselves why we are choosing one thing over another.

An educational choice that we are making at present is regarding piano lessons for our youngest. She would love to take piano lessons. The reality is Rebecca has learning disabilities. This does not automatically indicate piano lessons would be a bad thing. In fact, they would probably be very beneficial to her. The dilemma is in terms of the mental and emotional energy necessary to invest into her practicing time. She is fairly difficult to work with; the hours I spend each day with her often leave me weary and emotionally drained. To her credit, she works very hard, expending a lot of mental and emotional energy herself, just working against her learning disabilities to gain and retain what comes easily for most.

The question then begs to be asked, "Would the benefit of piano outweigh the additional drain to our emotional and mental reserves already taxed to the limit on a daily basis?" My gut response to this is no. If I go with my "no" I am then forced to let go of my desire for her to play piano, my desire to see her excel in something that taps into the beauty she so appreciates. And I must look the limitation full in the face, what is not going to be at this time, and I let it go. I choose to say no to piano, and as hard as that is, in that choosing I am saying yes to our relationship and the continued preservation of our mental and emotional energies, for this time and place in our lives.

These are the types of limitations we must often accept every time we make a choice. Yet it is in the accepting, embracing even, of limitations that we are free to live our lives as we choose.

List an educational choice you are presently facing:

_____

_____

_____

_____

What is the accompanying limitation of this choice?

_____

_____

Not reconciling ourselves to the limitations that each choice brings often leaves us with a lack of confidence regarding the choice made. A friend of mine calls this "choice regret," spending too much time mulling over the limit rather than being excited about the opportunity of the choice. We may even end up frozen and unable to make any choice at all. Any of these scenarios robs us of an inner strength and joy to walk confidently into the future. And whether the future is the next semester, the next school year or all the way into and through high school it would do us well to have a game plan well thought out—with as much attention given to what we are not choosing as to what we are in fact choosing.

In the following chapters we will be exploring more of the specific dynamics that influence and often determine what kinds of educational choices we make. A lot of our choosing we do intuitively, without hardly a thought. Yet the vast amount of material available for those who home school works in some ways against our intuition, as there is so much to process, so many pieces to any one decision, we are left overwhelmed.

As you let what you've read here settle within your own heart and mind and begin to see how the limitations of choice effect you more than you may have thought, keep in mind that the key to embracing and releasing the limitations that come with our choices is often a matter of grieving. Grieving may seem too "large" a word for our purposes here, "for it's only math curriculum" you may say. Yet is it really too "large" a word?

Haven't we all been educating our children with ideas and visions of what we'd like this to be about, how we'd like it to go? We all have our own favorite ways to learn for instance, but what if your child doesn't learn the same way? It is here where a simple grieving of what one expected, wished for, hoped for, serves to release the limitations for what they are, freeing our hands, hearts, and minds to receive the opportunities that come with choices we may never have naturally made.

Chapter Four
Family Realities

It is important as we plan our home schooling that we take our particular family's realities into account. It does us no good to ignore the dynamics that exist. We would not require a child with a broken arm to take swimming lessons; neither can we impose expectations upon ourselves and our children that are not compatible with the realities we live with. Some realities are short-term bumps in the road while others are more long-term, demanding greater reckoning.

Moving generates havoc
Death leads to emotional distress
Aging parents bring unpredictability
Financial struggles perpetuate inconsistency
Marital crisis leads to chaos
New babies result in topsy-turvy-dom
Illness brings exhaustion

All of these dynamics—whether they are regarded as a bump or a hurdle—must be allowed their place in our hearts, minds, and schedules. Our lives must therefore make room by setting aside something else for a time. Consider death for instance. It is a big hurdle and I'm pretty sure most of us would give allowance to it in our lives. However most of the realities of life have more subtle and intangible effects but are at the very least equally disturbing, and in fact are very often more troublesome because of the ways in which we choose to ignore and minimize their effects upon the lives of our children and ourselves.

A family reality of our own is that of learning disabilities. This has in fact thrown quite a curve ball into the way we educate our children. My youngest is the most severely affected, and the level of over-teaching and repetition that she needs in order to learn has had a rippling effect upon everyone else in the family. No longer do I have the time to spend with each child individually as spent at one time, nor do I have much brain power to put to the creative planning and choosing of studies, nor the dialogue or together type of learning that we once used to do. Our choices have been deeply impacted by the reality of learning disabilities and the resulting internal and external limitations imposed upon us.

Your family's unique realities impact you both internally and externally. It is easy to see external effects, especially in something like moving. Yet even here there would be internal realities that are easy to lose sight of in the midst of the external demands. When added to the task of moving a new baby, new job, new friends, or the lack thereof, you have a mountain of internal stresses compounding the sheer effort required to take down and set up house. It is foolish to home school without accepting reality for what it is. And reality would have it that we must occasionally lower our standards in one area of life that we may adequately deal with another. Here again we must choose what the focus of life is going to be about for this particular season.

Take a quick inventory of your life's realities at the present time. What is going on in your life at this time? What are the internal and external affects of each of these realities?

Reality (What is happening in life?)	External Effect (How is it affecting the logistics of life?)	Internal Effect (How is it affecting the hearts of you and your children?)

The Limitations

Now let's think of the limitation of our realities, for there are in fact limitations to what we can or cannot do depending on what we are dealing with in life. If learning disabilities are a reality you may not choose a relaxed style of educating. Long-term illness, whether in the life of a child or yourself is going to have an impact on what you choose to spend your precious time studying. New babies will determine the pace of your minutes, hours, and days. Marital crises will hamper the amount of creative and emotional energy you have to put into home schooling.

Reality (What is happening in your life?)	Limitations (What is not possible because of this reality?)

Juggling

One of the most helpful analogies to me over the years has been the idea of juggling. Often if not always there are too many balls to keep in the air. Even after sifting through who we are and what we value, there can be too many balls. The question must be asked, "Which balls are to remain in the air at this time, and which are to remain on the ground?" Far too often I found myself trying to keep them all in the air. But quite frankly there were too many to keep up at one time. We cannot do it all, and in education we cannot learn it all.

As moms we are responsible for caretaking: nurturing, comforting, advising, disciplining, and connecting with each child each day in ways unique to them and what speaks to them of love. We are responsible for the physical care and feeding of our children: laundry has to be done, clothing mended, sewn or purchased, picked up and put away. Food has to be purchased; meals made, served and cleaned up three times a day no less.

Our homes are to be havens of rest, places that speak of the heart of God. And so we decorate and then dust, arrange and then clean, set a standard and work to impart that same standard into the minds and hearts of our children. We buy, install, and then repair, mend and maintain all that is in our homes. And we have not yet mentioned the yard or garden that many of us have, or the ministry at church, volunteer service, or the friends we try to slot time for, or extended family which may or may not be a blessing in our lives, nor the part-time or full-time jobs many keep in order to help out with the cost of living.

And on it goes—far too many balls for one person at any given time. Add to this home schooling one, two, or more children and I wonder, "What are we thinking?"

In response to this dilemma, I began going before the Lord a number of years ago with this simple invitation, "God would You come into my day, our day? Would Your presence be here, and would You please show me which balls to juggle this day and which to let lie until another day."

In doing this I began to trust that He was in fact orchestrating my days that they would contain exactly the elements that I could deal with and in fact needed to be responsible for that day. But most of all I began to trust that the balls lying on the ground were okay to be there, that I didn't have to do it all in one day. I then began thinking of seasons of life in this way. And comfort with leaving a few balls on the ground for any given season of days began to be mine.

Schooling with the Seasons

Obviously a lot of life just doesn't afford us the luxury of being set aside for a day let alone days on end. If you don't feed your children you will find yourself answering to someone for your irresponsibility. And if your children are not very clean they will be shunned by other children who will pick up on the reality that they are not cared for, and therefore not worthy of being loved. And a home that is never tidied or cleaned will result in health hazards for yourself, your husband, and your children. I am not purporting we become sloppy in the basic responsibilities of life but I am suggesting that we take a good hard look at our expectations and really weed out the necessary from the ideal.

When we think of home schooling there are things that can be let go of for a time. Spelling doesn't have to happen every day of every year. Neither does grammar. Leaving things such as these for a time is not all bad. For just as the ground is rejuvenated after a season of lying fallow so can aspects of life find rejuvenation if left to lie for a time. Anything done too much or too long takes on the staleness of an old dry piece of bread. Yet let the dry activity lie and when once more picked up notice how refreshing it can be.

We used to have a membership to Science World and would regularly visit there. But after a few years Science World was no longer interesting to my children. So why bother any more? The whole trip cost us time, energy and money, and even though it was a great thing for a time, times change. And so do the seasons of a family's life.

Pause for Reflection

Jot down your expectations of self and children. (Consider your roles: chef, maid, Mrs. Fix-it, teacher, priest, lover ...)

Expectations for myself:

_____

_____

_____

_____

_____

Expectations of my children:

_____

_____

_____

_____

_____

In light of the realities of your life, which expectations do you think are realistic and which would you describe as unrealistic? Remember that what may have been realistic last year may not be this year, and what may not have been realistic before may very well be now.

As with the changing of the seasons, the changes in your family make this a good exercise to do on a regular basis. I'd suggest assessing your expectations at least once per year if not every semester.

Ask your husband and a good friend or two to read what you wrote and see if they would agree with you. Sometimes we think our expectations are too high because we are always met with frustration in a certain area when in fact the frustration may be the result of a job poorly done. So check it out with those you trust to speak honestly into your life.

Realistic expectations	Unrealistic expectations

The Stress Factor

As previously alluded to, home schooling families are not without our stresses. In fact we often create stress for ourselves. It is important as we assess our unique home schooling goals and realities that we ask ourselves some tough questions. Are we contributing to our own stress? Do we think that life is just happening to us?

Here are some further questions to think about. I suggest spending some time journaling your thoughts.

Which realities are negative and which are positive?
How am I contributing to my negative realities?
How are my negative realities affecting me internally?
Which realities do I have control over?
Which realities do I not have control over?
Have I or am I able to accept the limitations of my realities?
Are there any changes I need to make in order to live with my present realities?

Remember ...

When we choose we have not chosen something else.

X

Home schooling is like juggling
and some balls need to lie on the ground for a time.

X

Life is more manageable when:
We accept the responsibility of making choices,
Make those choices in light of our present realities;
And then accept the limitations of our choices.

Chapter Five
Learning Styles

Into the recipe of "us" comes learning styles, in short, the different ways in which we learn. Research has shown us that we are all pre-wired with what may be described as a learning value system; in other words, preferences for learning that supersede other avenues.

For instance, my husband Michael learns best by what passes through his eyes and not so much by what he hears. We could say that he values visual opportunities for learning and not auditory means. This is but one example. I learn and think best when I am holding a pencil in my hand. There is something about the kinetic connection between what my hand is doing and what my mind is able to retain. My daughter used to learn her multiplication tables by jumping up and down while reciting them. It made me dizzy just watching, but for her it was what she needed.

It is not only important to understand our children's learning styles, it is equally important to understand our own as well, since we usually teach in the style we ourselves are comfortable with. This is fine if our children thrive under our style—but this is certainly not always the case. Too often we become impatient with the ways our children learn that differ from our own. This need not be.

There are numerous books discussing learning styles, again each with its own lingo. Learning has been described as how we take in information, how we retain information, how we organize information, the different ways information sticks for each of us. Each author comes at the subject from a slightly different viewpoint; all offer valuable insight into the how and why of learning.

Of all the books available on learning styles my personal favorite is Thomas Armstrong's *In Their Own Way*. This book describes seven different learning styles: linguistic, logical-numerical, spatial, musical, body-kinesthetic, interpersonal, and intrapersonal. I recommend that you read his book to gain full understanding; in the meantime allow me to impart my own synopsis.

Learning Style	Characteristics
Linguistic	Learns by reading books, spelling words, word games, and thinking in words.
Logical/ Mathematical	Learns by forming concepts and looking for abstract patterns and relationships. Needs concrete materials to experiment with and lots of time to explore ideas.
Spatial	Learns visually, needs teaching through images, pictures, & color. Enjoys drawing & painting, 3-dimensional building, puzzles, Legos™ and map reading.
Musical	Learns through melody and rhythm.

continued

Learning Style	Characteristics
Body/ Kinesthetic	Learns by touching, manipulating and moving. Motivated through drama, role-play, and physical movement.
Interpersonal	Learns best by relating and cooperating through dynamic interaction with others. Enjoys group projects, community activities and games.
Intra-Personal	Learns best when left to himself. Enjoys opportunities to pursue independent study. Needs private space.

Can you see how different learning styles naturally lead to learning through different styles of study? Did you pick up on the catch words in each category which play a huge part in choices?

- Linguistic: thinks in words
- Logical/Mathematical: prefers concrete materials; needs time to explore new ideas
- Spatial: needs teaching through images
- Musical: through rhythm and melody
- Body/Kinesthetic: touching, manipulating, moving
- Interpersonal: dynamic interactions
- Intra-Personal: independent study

Just the differences between the first two, linguistic and logical/mathematical, are profound. The linguistic is an abstract thinker, while the logical mathematical values the manipulation of something concrete. Add to either one a spatial giftedness and you would have again two different kinds of learners. A linguistic/spatial would be able to "manipulate" abstract ideas in the mind, while a logical/mathematical/spatial would be able to "manipulate" objects in the mind.

We all have a combination of two, possibly more of these. But most likely there will be one dominant learning preference with a close second. This is where the differences are compounded. A linguistic learner who is also spatial will learn differently from a linguistic learner who is also musical. For the linguistic/spatial words will overlap images and language will be understood through images while images will need words put to them. For the linguistic/musical the language of life will be most meaningful when put to music and expressed through music. And music will bring understanding and an expression to life that words alone cannot do.

There are forty-nine possible combinations, each with a different avenue by which learning is not only accomplished but is full of zest and zing, learning that speaks of the best life has to offer.

Here is a smattering of how this works in our family:

Learning style	Family examples
Linguistic	• Mom: loves words, picky about words used • Danielle: gifted at language and speaking • Alexis: loves to read, enjoys colorful language
Logical/ Mathematical	• Rebecca: identifies patterns very quickly • Zachary: a math mind • Dad: learns best with concrete objects & circumstances
Spatial	• Zachary: excellent at map reading and directions • Rebecca: very good at puzzles • Mom: can manipulate objects and ideas in her head
Musical	• Justin: excels musically, writes music and lyrics • Rebecca: loves singing, has an excellent ear
Body/ Kinesthetic	• Alexis: expressive with body and face • Rebecca: touch aids memorization
Interpersonal	• Alexis: shares stories about people's lives, motivated by relationships • Zachary: people person, learns best in the company of others
Intra-Personal	• Justin: learns best by himself through reading • Danielle: likes to study independently

Read the questions and characteristics below in order to help understand where your children might fit.

Learning style	Some questions to help
Logical/ Mathematical	Does your child enjoy mentally computing math questions? Reason things out logically and clearly? Play chess, checkers, or other strategy games and win?
Spatial	Does your child spend free time in art activities? Easily read maps, charts, and diagrams? Enjoy jigsaw puzzles or mazes?
Musical	Does your child remember melodies? Tell you when a musical note is off key? Keep time rhythmically to music?
Body/ Kinesthetic	Does your child do well in sports? Move, twitch, tap, or fidget while sitting? Touch people when they talk to them?
Interpersonal	Does your child have a lot of friends? Enjoy group activities? Have a lot of empathy for the feelings of others?
Intra-Personal	Does your child display independence or a strong will? Seem to live in their own private world? March to the beat of a different drummer in their style of dress, behavior, or general demeanor?

Based on what you've discovered about learning styles place yourself and your children in the following table.

Learning style	Family examples
Linguistic	
Logical/ Mathematical	
Spatial	
Musical	
Body/ Kinesthetic	
Interpersonal	
Intra- Personal	

My two sons are as different as night and day. Let me show you how their learning preferences show up in their lives:

Justin's learning preferences	Description & examples
#1 Linguistic	• Loves reading and is a good writer • Is verbally expressive
#2 Musical	• Puts words into songs
#3 Intra-Personal	• Works best when left alone
SYNOPSIS: Justin learns best when given direction then left alone to complete assignments through reading and writing, preferably with music in the background.	

Zachary's learning preferences	Description & examples
#1 Mathematical	• Finds patterns of action & thought between subjects • Loves statistics
#2 Interpersonal	• Learns best when in the company of others
SYNOPSIS: The majority of Zachary's study needs to be done in the company of others, using values of community to make subjects meaningful.	

Notice that as we look at each child's learning preferences these actually reveal to us our children's values. It is not a stretch to venture that Justin values words and music that flow from within; whereas Zachary could be said to value community and topics which reflect relationships. Take time to record your own and your children's top two or three preferences and how this is expressed in life.

Learning preferences for: _____	Description & examples
#1	
#2	
#3	
SYNOPSIS:	

Learning preferences for: _____	Description & examples
#1	
#2	
#3	
SYNOPSIS:	

Learning preferences for: _____	Description & examples
#1	
#2	
#3	
SYNOPSIS:	

Learning preferences for: _____	Description & examples
#1	
#2	
#3	
SYNOPSIS:	

Learning preferences for: _____	Description & examples
#1	
#2	
#3	
SYNOPSIS:	

Time for Reflection

The concept of learning style is likely not new to you; however you may not have taken the time before to analyze your own style and how that plays out in your role as teacher. Equally important is how your teaching style is going to interface with your child's learning styles.

Consider these questions for a moment:

Have we been experiencing frustrations in our schooling that I now see are linked to style conflict?

What style elements do I need to incorporate into my curriculum choices to accommodate different styles? More music? More manipulatives? More pictures? More moving around?

When it comes to learning styles and choice we are blessed to have so many options of education open to us and to our children. As parents we are given opportunity to affirm the way our children learn by making choices based on their strengths. And this is one of the beautiful aspects of home schooling, being a blessing to our children as we learn about who they are and how they uniquely interact with the world about them. We do well as we embrace their unique learning styles, making educational choices for them and not against them.

Chapter Six
Personal Style

So far we have looked at home schooling methods, family realities, learning styles and what the ramifications of choice have on each of these. Identifying who we are as families would not be complete without discussing personal styles. Personal style is often described as personality or temperament. Whatever we call it, our style reflects the innate preferences of how we operate.

There are numerous books offering up their own brand of jargon and inventories on style. Many have come out of the business world and are useful for building efficient teams; others come from the counseling realm with a slant toward relationships and marriage. I will give generalized descriptions of some of the most popular and then go on to look at one man's definition of style in more detail and how we can apply that in our home schooling.

Ned Herman in the *Whole Brain Business Book* describes four quadrants of the brain and thus categorizes behavior as analyze, strategize, organize and personalize. Anthony Gregory speaks of two continuums, one being concrete vs. abstract, the other sequential vs. random. When these two continuums intersect, four quadrants, each with its own characteristics are formed. DISC is another four-quadrant model; its continuums describe people as task vs. people and process vs. quick. Another four-quadrant model by David Merril and Roger Reid emphasizes observable behavior as ask vs. tell, or controls emotions vs. emotes. And of course many of us are familiar with lion, beaver, otter and golden retriever as made popular by Gary Smalley. In addition to these is the popular Myers-Briggs sixteen personality types as well as the personality temperaments of melancholy, phlegmatic, choleric, and sanguine.

Consider Style, but with Caution

We all have a quadrant, style, or type in which we operate most easily and efficiently, and while terminology of temperaments is useful, we need to take caution in determining where our children fit. Children are still maturing and thus should not be assessed as though their behaviors are static. However we can begin to observe what appears to be preferences at fairly young ages. These harden into traits the older a child becomes.

Style becomes a tool to give understanding and to aid in acceptance of those who work differently from us. As moms it is very easy to slip into seeing our children as extensions of ourselves. They were in our wombs for nine months, entered the world through our bodies, and then seemed attached to the breast for ages. Because of physical realities of childbearing it takes us awhile to realize that they are not us and we are not them.

By the time my oldest had turned seventeen it became more and more apparent how very different we are, and this continues to amaze me. For instance, Alexis plans the night before what she will wear the next day, while I wait to see what I will feel like wearing. I could plan, but it would be a waste of time as I'll go by my response to the day at hand regardless of planning. I am the same with meals; even though I may do some planning, what I love most is to get to a mealtime and then respond to the time and mood at hand and prepare a meal accordingly. This drives Alexis to distraction. She used to ask what was for dinner at nine in the morning, to which I would have no other answer than "I haven't decided yet." We each find the other's style unfathomable and really cannot comprehend how the other works the way she does.

I began thinking of style and how it relates to home schooling when taking a course at our church about ministry passion, gifts, and styles. And this is the model I'll be sharing with you. Bruce Bugbee in his book *Network* uses the terms task vs. people and structures vs. unstructured in his description of style. There are those who are energized by tasks and those who are energized by people while how we are organized is described as structured or unstructured.

This is not to say that "task" people only ever do tasks and that "people" people only ever spend time with people, or that unstructured people are never structured or visa versa. But what it does mean is that we all have set preferences by which we are our best. A way to operate that energizes us and does not drain us.

Family Examples

I am wired task while my husband is wired people. I value getting a job done while his values are relationships and time spent in them and for them. To either of us it seems as though the other is unbalanced. He perceives me as all task and no relations while I perceive him as all relationship while tasks go undone.

Of course neither generalization or should I say oversimplification is true. For my husband does tasks while I do relationships. But, if given the choice of what either of us would get up for in the morning, this is our natural preference.

When I've had a particularly great day it is invariably because I've accomplished numerous tasks, while Michael would speak of a great day as having lots of connection between himself and others. Each of our children has a different preference. And the different home schooling styles will fit or not fit largely due to whether we are task or people oriented. In fact, many of the home schooling methods were spawned from the specific personal styles of their originators.

Charlotte Mason's style for instance, is easy to identify. The type of education bearing her name upholds high levels of interaction between educator and child. Learning is done in community with lots of dialogue and shared discovery. She obviously valued relationships and fashioned education around that. Independent learning is on the other end of the spectrum. By its very name we know it is done outside of people relationships. Every other home schooling method as described in Chapter Two would have its own place on the spectrum between task and people orientation.

My two boys personify each end of the task/people continuum. Justin works best alone with a task list that can be checked off as he goes. Zachary, on the other hand, loves to learn in the company of another. Taking either and trying to work against their set preferences not only results in frustration but in fact hampers if not stalls learning.

Unstructured versus structured speaks of how we organize life. Structured people like to have life happen in a routinely predictable way, while unstructured individuals work best when options are left open and the process by which to work has flexibility and options infused with spontaneity.

Here again we can see how home schooling styles each have their own place along the continuum between structured and unstructured. Textbook learning is often structured while unschooling is often unstructured. And so it is with us and our children and our predominant preferences as home schooling families. Each of us has a unique place on these continuums.

If we take the two spectrums and intersect them, we see that task or people individuals will each prefer structure or unstructured while structured or unstructured individuals will operate best under a task or people focus. Thus each quadrant has its own unique characteristics as seen on the following chart.

	Task-Oriented (gains energy from accomplishing a goal)	People-Oriented (gains energy from interacting with people)
Structured	• *enjoys getting a job done* • *likes to focus on results* • *likes following agendas* • *comfortable with clear goals & how to accomplish a task*	• *likes defined relationships* • *secure in familiar surroundings* • *desires stable & defined settings*
Unstructured	• *likes general guidelines* • *likes versatility* • *enjoys tangible results* • *likes a variety of responsibilities*	• *appreciates spontaneous situations* • *very conversational* • *relates well to others* • *very flexible*

Bill Kuhn and Steve Wille in their internet essay entitled "Stop Trying to Fix People" make this point. They write: "There are two ways to build a low-performance team: emphasize your own style and invalidate all other styles."

As home schoolers it is far too easy to make our own style the mandate of our homes. Yet this prohibits the emerging style preferences of our children. This does not validate who they are or instill an inherent confidence in their uniqueness and the need the world has of what they have to offer.

Style is as individualized as a fingerprint. In order to make use of our own and others' uniqueness we must become comfortable with the tension present due to the differences. We often want life to be "nice", and sometimes we try to create this by erasing differences in each other, or at least minimizing them. But this leads to individuals being invalidated and actually works against the very thing that we are working towards, namely community. We forget that in all things there is tension which holds the sum of the parts together as a whole. This is true in the physical world and it is true in the world of relationships. Every good team is comprised of people with strengths in all four quadrants, with each working out of their strengths, thereby resulting in greater efficiency and productivity, not to mention creativity.

How does this apply to home schooling? I'll use my son Zachary as an example. As mentioned before he is people-oriented. I occasionally try to tell him to do his work in his room, but it is generally unsuccessful. Forcing him to operate as a task person would actually rob him of energy. This energy lost then leaves him bereft of the motivation needed to do the work his studies require of him.

We can think of ourselves as a battery. Batteries need to be charged in order to work. They require energy to give out energy. If we are only doing those things that drain energy from us then our lack of energy will become evident in other areas of life.

I am a much better mom when I am getting some concrete tasks done. Tasks give me the energy needed to interact personally with my husband and children. If all I am doing is people stuff I am very quickly drained and am left feeling depleted with "'nothing to give".

For my son Zachary it is the opposite. In order to attend to his necessary tasks he needs recharging through personal interaction with others. And it isn't difficult to see how our opposing value systems can come into conflict and how, if I try to fit him into the way I work, he is left feeling hurt and invalidated.

It can be quite challenging when a parent is the opposite style to that of the child. For instance, an unstructured child in a structured home may feel claustrophobic and boxed in, resulting in rebellion. Conversely a structured child with an unstructured parent may feel insecure and unsure about life. I have personally struggled with this dynamic. I am an unstructured person with three of my children needing structure.

At times it is very easy to feel defeated because it seems that I cannot give them as much structure as they need. Yet, I must ask myself, "In what ways can I give them structure?" I then do what I can. On the other hand for a structured parent with an unstructured child the question would be, "In what ways can I give my child the spontaneity they crave?" Let's not get stuck in the downward spiral of becoming victims to our own and others' personalities. Rather let's celebrate our diversity, and understanding personal styles is one way to accomplish this.

Place your family members into the following table:

	Task-Oriented	People-Oriented
Structured		
Unstructured		

There will be families who home school in a very structured way and those who are very unstructured. Neither is any more wrong or right than any other way. The questions to consider are: "Does the way we prefer really support the children we are home schooling? Do we know who we are? Do we know our preferences? Do we know our children's preferences?" Here again, we are not to home school as others do, but to be responsible for ourselves and to God in that process.

What specific challenges have you encountered in your home schooling due to opposing personal styles?

_____

_____

_____

_____

_____

Answer whichever of the following best fits your reality.
  -In what ways can I give my children more structure?
  -In what ways can I give my child the flexibility they need?

_____

_____

_____

_____

_____

Energy: think of each child and how they are energized and what robs them of energy. Then compare this with how you are home schooling.
  -Does the method fit for each child?
  -Where could the way I home school use some tweaking?

_____

_____

_____

_____

_____

We all want our children to be motivated. And one of the common frustrations of home schooling is in motivating our children. But what we often really want is to know how to motivate our children to live and operate by our preferred style, meanwhile wondering why they are not motivated.

And something to think about is that far too often we turn into discipline issues what is merely a style difference. It may be as difficult and as simple as allowing for, making room for, and even embracing our children's styles as different as our own.

For Reflection

Understanding personality styles can bring tremendous freedom in all our relationships because we are free to accept others for the way God made them and the contributions they bring to the family, committee, team, and office, without judging them or being frustrated with them for being different from ourselves.

What caught your attention in this chapter?
What new things did you learn about yourself and your children?

_____

_____

_____

_____

_____

_____

_____

_____

_____

Chapter Seven
Skills & Knowledge

As we determine goals for each semester there are two facets of education that can be taken into account: skills and knowledge. H. Clay Trumbull in his book, *Hints on Child Training*, says:

> Teaching gives knowledge. Training gives skill. Teaching fills the mind. Training shapes the habits. Teaching brings to the child that which he did not have before. Training enables a child to make use of that which is already his possession. We teach a child the meaning of words. We train a child in speaking and walking. We teach him truths which we have learned for ourselves. We train him in habits of study, that he may be able to learn other truths for himself. Training and teaching must go on together in the wise upbringing of any and every child. The one will fail of its own best end if it be not accompanied by the other. He who knows how to teach a child is not competent for the oversight of a child's education unless he also knows how to train a child."

If we accept H. Clay Trumbull's edict regarding skills and knowledge as insightful and accurate, then it would have to be realized that we would be training different children different skills. For what would be a skill to train in one child would be knowledge to be taught to another.

For instance: I have a daughter who is a natural at public speaking. This would then become a skill I am to train in her. Conversely I have a son who is not a natural at public speaking. This would then be an area in which I teach him how to speak in public. Do you see the difference?

"Teaching brings to the child what he did not have before. Training enables a child to make use of what is already his possession."

Some will have natural affinities for science, others for history. One will have a knack for math while another for writing. As parents we have opportunity to train what our children are naturally gifted at while teaching those weaker areas, shoring up so to speak other areas of life and living that they may not choose if left to their own devices. In planning our educational goals what is important to know "in this semester" and "for this child" is what the focus is going to be; either training or teaching because the resources used for each is different.

If I have a child who has naturally well developed fine motor skills coupled with a sharp eye for details I would not really need to teach per se that child to write well. But I could train the natural affinity of penmanship into a real work of art by providing access to calligraphy materials and such. Conversely a child who struggles with fine motor skills is going to need a lot more technical and specific instruction, augmented by more review most likely in the form of writing handbooks. Where one type of handwriting resources becomes redundant if a natural skill is already there so that same resource becomes invaluable for another who could benefit from "teaching" through repeated practice.

When my eldest daughter, Alexis, was four years old we were discussing the story of David & Goliath. I asked her why she thought David killed Goliath, her answer was, "Because he refused to follow God's ways." Her answer revealed a natural affinity for a depth of perception not readily shown by all four year olds. This perception is then something that is my privilege to train. In others of my children it would be necessary to teach a perception in thinking as it is not a natural affinity within them; it is not a "something which they already possess."

And so it would be with all of the knowledge and skills we desire our children to have. Some we are to teach and others to train.

Following is a list of skills and knowledge. This list is by no means comprehensive, and within each there would be subcategories of knowledge and skills. As you read through make notes about which are natural affinities in your children and which are definitely not.

critical thinking

memorization skills

time management

self discipline

organizing one's thoughts

reading to learn

following directions

study skills

habits pertaining to character

public speaking

research skills

money management

penmanship

sportsmanship

etiquette and manners

government/civic responsibility

geography

history

sciences

Christian world view

religion

ecosystems

music

drama

measurements

geometry

math

social intelligence

emotional intelligence

spelling

grammar

computer skills

writing styles

keyboarding

life skills (cooking, laundry, tidiness, and more)

Child's Name	Natural Affinities (what my child already possesses)	Limitations (what is really not there)

Synopsis:

Synopsis:

Synopsis:

Synopsis:

Synopsis:

In applying choice in our decisions of with what and how to educate each of our children I've a simple formula to keep in mind. Never train skills with difficult information; when newly training a skill use easily assimilated knowledge. Conversely if you are teaching difficult information, allow the student to learn it using skills in which they are confident. Teaching a difficult subject as well as training new skills is only going to frustrate and take the joy out of learning, and it could send into hiding the very skills our children have a natural affinity for.

$$\text{New Skill + Difficult Information} = \frown$$
$$\text{New Skill + Familiar Information} = \smile$$
$$\text{Familiar Skill + New Information} = \smile$$

Part of my role in the education of my children is to bring them up in habits of success. There will always be places of failure and for sure they need to learn how to deal with failure as much as success. The thing is that habits of success (and failure) have a way of increasing exponentially in our lives. And if I can balance teaching and training in the lives of my children with an eye to success in what they are doing, that will in time reap its own rewards.

It is quite possible to educate my child in an attitude of contrariness, where everything they do is not quite good enough. And I could make it all the more difficult, essentially setting them up for failure, by insisting that skills being newly developed must march alongside new and advanced knowledge, confounding their best intentions and heart's desire to do well.

What Choosing Between New Skills, New Information Can Do

It is as I determine the focus for each unit, semester, or year that choices can be made about the focus for each child. Will the focus for this week be skill training in the midst of knowledge, or will the focus be new knowledge in the context of skills in which she is confident? If for a time I choose skill training over new knowledge, here again I will have to reconcile myself to what I am choosing not to do.

My youngest in her progress through math is on the cusp of entering the world of fractions and decimals. These will be new concepts for her. She has a math mind, yet it has been confounded due to her vulnerabilities to overload, the struggle to organize information in her mind, as well as significant naming difficulties, all aspects of the learning disabilities with which she struggles. So the choice for the next few weeks is to give her the time to firm up her knowledge of multiplication and division facts before going on. For if she is presented with a new concept (skill) before the knowledge (facts) of the last concept is firm, we will most likely need to retrace our steps at some point in this march through math, and we actually cannot afford the time to do that. Taking the time now will in fact save time, not to mention emotional and mental stress, in the future.

This does present a certain limitation and subsequent choice. For me the choice is to take it slow and steady, but that also means that for a few weeks' time it will feel as though she is not progressing in math concepts. The challenge is to rest easy in that limitation and the feeling of being behind the eight ball, choosing to delay for a time one aspect of her education that her energies, mental and emotional, be focused on the task of memorization, something that has never come easy to her.

Deciding on a focus for each unit of time does not mean that skills will be trained to the exclusion of all knowledge being taught, or that knowledge will be taught to the exclusion of all skills being trained. For knowledge is often the "road" by which skills are trained and skills are often the "road" by which knowledge is taught. For example, learning the timeline of the Middle Ages trains the skill of memorization while the skill of research enables a child to produce a report about what she knows. And so it goes, back and forth between skills and knowledge.

Embracing Limitations, Embracing Privileges

This dance between skills and knowledge is largely based on an intuition of our child's strengths and weaknesses and how she intersects with the lessons of education. And this is where my own education takes place. I too am learning the skills of teaching while becoming familiar with the knowledge of the education I desire my child to have. And as I become more adept in the skills and knowledge of education I can pass on an education wrapped in an increasing depth and perception about life and who we are; learning to rest in our choices, resting in our limitations, making wise choices according to who we are.

Every time we look at the knowledge to be taught it is good to know what skill we are seeking to train through the teaching. Our children need to be provided with the skills and knowledge that best serves them as individuals at any given time in their development. As we reconcile ourselves to the limitations of choice we will be more equipped to take on the responsibility and privilege of providing an education that is specially suited to each child; an education rich in knowledge and skills.

Chapter Eight
Responsibility Quotient

As we set educational goals it is important to assess how much responsibility each child is ready to assume. Being a mom of five children I am eager to pass on the responsibility of learning to my children. Yet doing so is not always appropriate and in fact may be downright harmful if done too soon.

Passing the torch of responsibility I find similar to weaning. Let's not misunderstand the purpose of weaning our children in regards to their studies. It is not to release us from the responsibility of providing an education. It merely takes one or more dimensions of their learning out of our hands so that our time as teacher and parent can be directed to another facet of their education. It's handing over the responsibility of one task so that we can assume the responsibility of another.

The education of our children includes not only their book work but in a broad sense general life skills. With our five children I was always aware of how many could tie their shoes and how many were left to learn. Or how many could pump on the swing by themselves, and how many still were to get it. All through the years it was a "three down, two to go" sort of tallying. And what that tallying meant to me was the increased independence of my children and less dependence on me. And with five young ones that always seemed like good news.

Small Steps to Independence

Teaching a child how to pump on a swing is a combination of time spent, explicit instruction, and waiting; they all get it sooner or later. But in the arena of "schooling" it isn't so easy to understand how to pass on increasing independence, as there are often many parts that work towards independence. For instance, let's work through a scenario of what it would be like for your child to do his vocabulary workbook by himself.

1. First he needs to know where his workbook is kept and be able to find it when needed.
2. Then he needs to be able to open it to the appropriate page.
3. Following that he needs to read to learn and follow directions.
4. Finally he needs to answer the questions in the workbook without input from you.
5. The culmination? Doing all of this without you being in the same room.

Did you notice how many little steps there are in accomplishing that one goal? So when you begin to wean, do it very slowly, in incremental steps. Again, make sure the actual study is at a level where your child can succeed for the real lesson is independence from mom. If in the midst of learning independence you assign a difficult subject matter you will frustrate your child and yourself. Once your child has learned that it is possible to be independent you can then increase the difficulty of the subject matter. Albeit, keep in mind that educating our children is a dance. This necessitates that we walk the fine line of drawing close in teaching and assisting, then drawing away in order to teach first of all confidence then independence within that confidence.

If we give the child responsibility for his education too soon we set him up for frustration at best, failure at worst. Interestingly enough holding back or waiting too long to impart independence ultimately results in the same consequences, frustration and failure.

John Taylor Gatto describes the ages of thirteen and fourteen as the years of boldness and a sense of invincibility within the child. Instead of fighting this dynamic in our early adolescents let's harness this drive and use it to propel our children into the very characteristics by which we define adulthood.

Authority, Responsibility and Privilege

In order to do this there is a fundamental principle which must be understood: authority, responsibility and privilege go hand in hand. Whether it is in education, home life, or the working world, these realities must be kept in balance. As adults we have many responsibilities and we also have much authority and privilege. When the principle of keeping these in balance is not respected havoc results in the hearts and minds of those involved.

For example, consider a man working for a boss where he is given responsibility without the authority needed to get the job done. Or consider a woman who is given the responsibility of buying groceries for her family but is not given the authority to decide what, when, where, or how much to buy. Both these examples reflect a stripping of one's personal power by another.

As an adult I am able to reject responsibility if it does not carry the authority necessary to get the job done. Our children on the other hand are innocent of this principle and are therefore more vulnerable to its abuses. And that is where moms and dads are called to protect. Sometimes it is from us and our own mismanagement of life that they need protection.

Responsibility Deserves a Degree of Authority and Privilege

I first became aware of this principle at the age of fourteen. My mom was a working mom and I had the job of cooking dinners. I remember having my cooking utensils out ready to use in whatever I was cooking. My mom would come home and promptly put away whatever utensils were out. I had been given the responsibility of cooking dinner yet was not allowed the authority to decide how and with what to do that. This is a very simple example of how this works.

Russia's communist system tried for seventy-one years to give responsibility without authority or privilege. While we could easily see the results on the psyche and morale among the people who lived under that regime, it is much more difficult to clearly see the subtle ways we can do the very same things with our children.

Following are a few of the concrete ways this principle can work in the lives of our children.

Situation	Responsibility	Authority	Privilege	When an aspect is missing
Young child grocery shopping with mom	To obey & cooperate with mom	Control over own actions	Being able to go shopping with mom	If the child can't handle the responsibility of obeying and cooperating with mom, then the privilege of shopping should be removed
Older child grocery shopping with mom	To not nag at mom to buy this and that	Control over tongue and actions	Pushing their own buggy & being sent to other parts of the store for items on mom's list	
Getting book work done	To do the required work	Authority to decide either how, when, where, possibly what	The opportunity to choose, to have some say	If the child is given responsibility without any sense of authority, we leave them with no sense of ownership & no reason to care
Child setting the table	Responsibility to set the table properly	Being able to set & decorate the table as they choose	Privilege of a personal touch	
Child cooking	To cook a meal for the family	Authority to decide when & how to serve the meal	Privilege of personal touch & choice of meal	
Younger child staying home with an older child	Younger child must respect older as having authority from parents	Control over own actions	Getting to stay home vs. whatever else	If the younger child cannot handle having authority over own actions then that child is not ready to stay with an older child, as it is not the older child's responsibility to control the younger
	Older child must treat younger child with care, not lording authority	Caretaking of younger siblings, protecting them from harm	To be in charge, to be trusted, opportunity to learn responsibility	

These are just a few simple and basic ways that the balance of authority, privilege, and responsibility work out in very tangible ways in the lives of our children. There are obviously numerous more scenarios that we could discuss, for the principles are in every area of our lives.

Take a bit of time to consider how this principle is properly or perhaps improperly applied in your own home, just to get a feel for how it works. Consider your own responsibility/authority ratio in your family situation. Are they in reasonable balance? In which direction do you tend to lean: more toward responsibility or more toward privilege?

Situation	Responsibility	Authority	Privilege	When one aspect is missing

Back to Johnny and his workbook. How does it look to implement responsibility, authority, and privilege in the educating of our children? How do we use this principle to guide us as we slowly hand over the technical aspects of education into our children's hearts and hands?

I use the principles of authority and responsibility as gauges of maturity. If I am giving an assignment that my child is able to responsibly finish on time, then I know I might be able to increase his authority surrounding that task. For instance, if my son is doing his grammar workbook in a timely fashion then I will loosen the hold on the time frame in which it is done. This would be the difference between expecting grammar to be done by lunchtime as compared to so much done by the end of the week, or so much done by Wednesday and more by Saturday.

If upon proceeding to do this he is still accomplishing his grammar in a timely fashion then I know he is able to handle the increased authority of managing his own time. If I loosen the timeframe in which the workbook is expected to be completed and he is not able to manage his time so as to finish in a timely fashion, in other words the work is not getting done when it is supposed to be, then I take that as a clue to step back and reinstate more structure about when to do his grammar book, again bringing him to a place where he can be successful.

In this way I use this principle to gauge what to put into my child's hands and what to maintain as my own as far as responsibility and authority. And I find it quite naturally works out that as my children increase in the amount of authority they are able to carry that privilege just becomes a natural outflow of increased authority and responsibility. It is not very often that I have to manufacture privilege, although it certainly doesn't hurt to once in a while throw in rewards here and there as tangible tokens of a job well done and of maturity gained.

Chapter Nine
Putting it Together

When a family just begins to home school it is usually the mom who asks around about what kind of curriculum or program to use. And there is always lots of advice and "I just found this math program, it's great, you should go with it." And of course she hears this sort of thing from every corner into which she asks. Whether this leaves the family feeling good about their choices made or just overwhelmed is actually not the point. The point is that the recommendations of her friends and acquaintances may not be the "best" for her particular family.

I have found home schooling to be a faith journey but also a journey of instinct. It takes time to attune one's instincts to what home schooling is, for others and then for yourself. And in the meantime we very easily fall prey to "this is the best, you should go with it."

Too many parents struggle for years finding the "right" curriculum or program for their family only to realize at some time, perhaps years down the road, that it wasn't quite right. Why do you think that the home schooling market is so very large and well stocked? Partly because there is just a lot of very good material out there, while another dynamic fueling this business is one of demand.

In past days demand was a good thing in that it spurred people on to produce quality material for home schoolers and we have all reaped the benefits of this. But I wonder if today the demand is not merely a struggle to find what "fits". And so we keep producing and buying more and more, wondering why what was "great" for Sally is not so great for me.

It boils down to family dynamics, most of which we have already discussed. Yet the discussion of these dynamics is not for mere understanding only. It does us no good to say, "One of my sons is an interpersonal learner and the other is an intra-personal learner" if I actually do not make curriculum choices based on this knowledge and understanding.

Standing Apart

The difficulty of this is not in the lack of material or a style of home schooling to fit each individual, the challenge is in the peer pressure we put on each other. For if I really pay attention to my family's realities, at this time, I then may very well (most likely) be doing something very different from what any number of my home schooling friends and acquaintances are doing. And the reality is that they may not understand, and I will have to stand apart from the very people who are an integral piece of my support network. And this can be a difficult thing to do.

Home schoolers are a very eclectic lot. All you have to do is look around and listen to the women in your support group to see this; and we are also all very sure of ourselves most of the time. The problem comes when we take our surety and try to make it another's by pressuring that other to home school the way we do it, or to use "this great curriculum" because we have had so much success with it.

This is sheer arrogance. We must look at the individual needs and realities of the family and take that into account. Each family has a mother and a father with different family backgrounds, with different value systems, and different learning styles, teaching styles, and just plain different rhythms of living. I never did mention the difference it makes to home schooling being a night or morning person, did I? This makes a huge difference, and one that will affect the type of curriculum or program that you choose and whether it will actually work for your family or not.

And of course each family has a differing number of children with differing personalities within those children. Not to mention the numerous limitations evident within each one of us. What is the answer when I have children who need structure and I am not structured? I mentioned before that this has been a huge reality in our lives. And part of the reason my children need structure is that we are dealing with a very strong family base of learning disabilities. And children with learning disabilities need structured learning. They actually don't thrive well under what my ideal of home schooling was when I started; that being, "Let me read a book to you, we'll look at a map about what we read, we'll find some additional references and material about an aspect of what we read about and hey, let's add this to our timeline, then later we'll do some writing about what struck us, add something to our lap book, and we'll fit some math in after lunch."

The Reality

Our reality is so far from this it isn't even funny. Actually this did work for quite a few years, until I was doing five grades at once and realizing that a couple of mine were just not "catching on" like some of the others did. And of course this sent me on a journey of discovery, and of networking with others struggling with learning disabilities and of buying more direct instruction resources to aid my children to learn what many children learn through seeming osmosis.

During that time one of the math curriculums I tried was Saxon Math. Now Saxon Math is a great math resource, very thorough, very academically sound. But what I didn't realize is that it is a language-based resource, and with children struggling with language-based learning disabilities you can see how this just didn't mesh with who we are. So we basically wasted a couple of years of math and quite a bit of money, not to mention the emotional struggle of trying to make this particular math curriculum work. And I still have some Saxon Math books for sale if you'd like them!

After about eight years of home schooling I stopped running after the "latest and best" thing. And I just began to "dig my heels in" and get down to business. And business meant beginning our home schooling day at 7:00 in the morning, continuing through each child assessing their assignments done and those to do, teaching whatever was needed at the time, basically tutoring one on one, finishing off by about 3 p.m. each day. My children were not doing seven plus hours of schooling per day, but I was. And this worked for a number of years, mostly because I said "no" to a lot of stuff, and because I became very diligent and focused, and yes, structured. By the way, home schooling is the best character development program I've ever encountered.

This is what I had to do at the time. Why? Because I had five children, all at different grade levels and abilities, combined with learning disabilities and all the challenges of that. They just plain needed one-on-one direct instruction. So this all sounds very responsible and like I was some kind of wonder woman, and the general response of women when they hear this is to either bow in worship or faint in despair of "That's what its going to be?" Well maybe and maybe not. Quite frankly if I had two children who did not struggle with learning disabilities and who were quick and eager learners I would home school very differently. I would not carry on an insane schedule, nor would I give a lot of direction, as quick and eager learners are those who often create and maintain their own learning.

Schooling to Fit the Situation

Now take out the quick and eager learner reality and consider two children who do not struggle with learning disabilities and home schooling would again look quite different. I would probably be a bit more deliberate with our lessons, but again the reality of what that would exactly look like would depend on more factors not yet taken into account. Such as: are they both girls and boys or one of each? Boy learning is generally different from girl learning but not always. My one son fits the girl's way of learning while my other is all boy. So, it's conceivable you could have one boy and one girl who learn the same way and it flows great.

This was our reality when I started. My first two children, a boy and a girl, loved me reading aloud. And so we snuggled on the couch and read and read and read. My third and fifth children are the ones struggling with auditory processing deficits and cannot therefore follow a story when it is read aloud to them. My fourth child, a girl, hates stories. She has a mind like a scientist and just does not enjoy stories about anything. Thus reading aloud fell flat on its face.

So what's a mom to do? Well, you change. You grieve the limitations and the realities of what you had expected in comparison to what you actually have and you get on with the educating of your children as they need it. Not as you would have it, not as others educate their children, not with the materials that others use, but with what your family's personality demands. And that means assessing curriculum and program choices with a very discerning eye and a careful hand. It also means trusting your gut more.

Respecting Parents' Intuition

One of the logics given regarding home schooling is that parents know best. We know our children better and thus parents are the best choice in the education of our children. We generally resist home schooling in a way which mimics what is done in the marketplace of education, preferring to create a different, more free, more structured, or more (you fill in the blank) model of education.

What must be remembered is that within the general model of home schooling diversity abounds, primarily because of the intuition of the parents involved. We must put back into the hands and hearts of home schooling families a confidence that they do know their child best and can make worthy decisions based on that; a confidence in their gut, not my gut, not another's gut, but their gut. I am not suggesting that we don't need networking for we need it desperately. But there is a fine line of support for the intuition of another and the knocking down of that same person's intuition.

Granting One Another Freedom to be Out of the Box

As a home schooler I pride myself on thinking out of the box, of living out of the box. So what happens when those of us who are out of the box just make for ourselves other boxes to live in and then surreptitiously impose those boxes on the unsuspecting yet like-minded home schooling women and families about us. We are actually shooting ourselves in the foot, undermining the very strengths upon which home schooling has been built ... the confidence that as a parent I know my child best, that I have an instinct for and about my child, that I have what it takes to educate my child, until such time that I may not. But that I can then take even what I lack to God above and trust Him for His very specific revelation and provision.

If this book does nothing else I hope it gives wisdom in assessing who our families are, who we are not, and living educational lives that fit us as individual units. It is sad the amount of peer pressure to conform to the latest new curriculum or resource. Again, the resources out there are for the most part great. But great can be a pretty relative term, because great on its own and great in light of my child and our dynamics may very well be two different things. What is great, when standing by itself, may in fact be not so great when combined with our personal family's dynamics and realities.

I see grace being given to the home schooling community in two ways. First we give it to ourselves, trusting our own instincts and knowledge of who we are. Secondly we grant the same to those around us.

I have a friend who began home schooling a few years ago. And she did some networking asking others what they were using and would recommend. And she asked me as well. Her comment at the time is very telling. She said that I was the only person who did not tell her exactly what to use, as in "use this, it's great." I think she really appreciated that I did not pressure her with the choices I had made for my family. I didn't tell her "Math-U-See was exactly what my oldest needed. You should go with that." Instead I asked questions: "How does Jordan learn? Does he like doing workbooks, or does he enjoy manipulative sort of learning?"

It turns out he loves doing workbooks, so that's pretty easy when it comes to math, get a good workbook. "But don't bother with Math-U-See, that would make you the teacher and that is not what you or he needs."

"What about reading, how is he learning that?" It turns out that Jordan just reads ... very little phonics, very little instruction and he reads. Okay, so what that tells me is that I am not going to suggest *Spell to Write and Read* or *The W.I.S.E. Guide for Spelling* by Wanda Sanseri. These resources have been fabulous for a number of my children but for my friend this would be redundant. It would bog them down in stuff they don't need to be doing, in spite of the fact that these are excellent resources.

Because of Jordan's love of workbooks they got a workbook that introduces phonics as part of a comprehensive language arts program. He does learn it, yet without the direct formal instruction, i.e.: whiteboard, specific process, much repetition with frequent review and assessment that was so necessary with my own children.

The thing is, we've got to give each other tools of strength and must accept these same tools for ourselves; namely taking home schooling back to a journey of instinct and faith. Both go beautifully hand in hand. There are so many truly beautiful ways to home school as well as plenty of fabulous resources out there.

A Journey of Hope, Faith and Discovery

We need to read the books, glean from others' wisdom, take from journeys of success and journeys of failure, learning what worked and what hasn't worked from those around us. And then we take all that knowledge, all those ideas, and all the options available in the education of our children—then we quiet our own hearts and minds, filtering out all of the voices around us, allowing the peripheral of what we've heard fall away—basically the chaff in regards to our particular family and home schooling realities. Then we keep the good stuff, the useful stuff. Not my friends' useful stuff, not the useful stuff of the woman we may admire so much, but the stuff that is "good" for us, for who we are, me and my children and our household. And then we take those pieces, turning them into a plan, and then we work the plan. Plans will always need tweaking from time to time, but that's okay. The whole thing is a journey of discovery—just as much a discovery of who we are as a discovery of the world about us.

For the remainder of this book I'll be sharing with you a tangible way to take the personal realities of your family and how to interface them with your intended topic of study. Even within the plan for planning that I'll be sharing—trust your gut and tweak where you need; none of it need be static. So, enjoy the process.

Chapter Ten
Making Your Plan: An Introduction

When my children were young, I needed a study plan that I could put down and pick up as needed. For with many little ones there are as many unexpected quiet moments as chaotic ones. And it is good to have a response to each moment as it comes. Therefore it is always handy to have your study plan in your back pocket, ready to be whipped out at a moment's notice, while the little one is napping, while the toddler is off with Grandma for an unexpected outing, while the house is in relatively good order so mom's mind is free to fly on the wings of learning … you get the picture.

This next set of chapters will help you to organize your choices into a management system. I intend to show you how to organize your schooling:
- step by step
- in a way which allows you to plan as you have the time
- incorporating all subjects
- by providing a filter for choices to pass through

Because of the busyness of life, we need to organize in a way that does not depend on having a weekend, or even a day to set aside for planning. While seeking a solution to my own time challenges a process of organizational steps began to evolve, steps that can be done one at a time, leaving and then returning, still knowing what has been accomplished and what the next step is. This process or system of organization allows for planning a semester's study in pockets of time. It encourages the inclusion of literature, art, writing, hands-on activities, language study, Bible, as well as field trips. It's a system which ties curriculum, multiple resources, and your own idea into a unified whole. Whether you desire to organize a small part of your school year at a time, a semester at a time or even the whole year, the same process applies. In order to understand where we are going, let me present an overview of the management steps.

Step 1

In Step One you have opportunity to analyze your family goals, styles and needs in relationship to your next semester's study focus, taking the time to discern where you are and where you want to head.

Step One: Making an Assessment
- Goals
- Styles
- Needs

Step 2

Step Two provides opportunity for overview, brainstorming and detailing of all the books, resources and curriculum you may desire to use. A big picture of the next semester's "personality" is what Step Two should provide.

Step Two: Brainstorming
• Overview
• Brainstorming
• Detailing

Step 3

Step Three is for categorizing our lists from Step Two. This is especially helpful if you have older and younger students, as you may discover you have plenty of materials for one age bracket and not the other. Step Three gives opportunity to weed out duplicate or redundant resources, simplifying your lists and expectations. This saves time later on.

Step Three: Categorizing Resources
• Categorizing (younger/older)
• Weeding out the unnecessary, identifying holes
• Simplifying

Step 4

Step Four is for determining the length of your semester while deciding the semester's outline. Here we combine your real-life schedule with what you want to accomplish academically, making sure your goals remain realistic and able to fit into life.

Step Four: Semester Length & Outline
• Determine length of unit
• Mesh real life with academic expectations

Step 5

Step Five creates a Weekly Outline. Here you begin to delegate resources and applicable goals or parts thereof to their own week. This is done based on your outline as determined in Step Three.

Step Five: Weekly Outline
• Weekly outcome
• Delegate resources/goals specifically

Step 6

Step Six finds us specifying further, breaking the Weekly Outline of Step Five into Daily Outlines. This step is not necessary if you desire to work task-to-task throughout the week from Step Five's Weekly Outline. But Step Six will leave you with daily tasks if you'd like.

Step Six: Daily Outcome
• Daily outlines/tasks

Step 7

In Step Seven we create assignment sheets for our children. Assignments are based on the specific weekly goals laid down in Step Five. Through this we endeavor to begin passing the baton of educational responsibility to our children.

Step Seven: Assignment sheets
• Assignment sheets

In my opinion one of the greatest blessings of home schooling is the freedom to find one's rhythm of living. And a well planned course of study supports the flow of life by not railing against it, but rather softly coming alongside asking to be let in. So let's begin.

Chapter Eleven
Step One: Making an Assessment

Now that you have determined your overall educational goals, looked at your family's styles, and your realities have been assessed, you are in a position to apply this information to what you would like to study. In other words use that information to filter your intended study.

Taking the time to accurately interpret what each study has to offer allows for us to respond with what we can bring to each study. For example when we studied Ancient Rome I first identified the knowledge that Ancient Rome had to offer. I filtered that knowledge through the maturity level and ages of my children. Automatically some of the knowledge available was set aside as unnecessary and inappropriate considering their ages.

What a Study of Rome Offers	Children's Ages	Chosen Study Areas
Who? What? When? Where?	one, three, five, seven, & nine	Who? What? When? Where?
Government & Administration		
The Effect of Beliefs on Culture		The Effect of Beliefs on Culture
Religion / Paganism		
War		
The Collapse of an Empire		
Arts & Architecture		Arts & Architecture

We then applied our family's styles to the knowledge available within our chosen focus areas. This determined the best ways to assimilate the information. I asked, "What do our unique styles or needs contribute to or ask of this study?" I then determined what skills needed to be learned and determined if and how this study could facilitate the training of those skills.

A) What the study offered (knowledge to be gained):
- Who, what, when, where
- Effects of beliefs on culture
- Arts and architecture

PLUS

B) What we brought to the study (styles, maturity levels, unique needs):
- Artistic ability

- Unstructured teaching style
- Interest in stories, listening skills
- The need for something that can be done in small pockets of time as toddler is disruptive

PLUS

C) What skills we needed to learn (skills I needed to train):
- Narration
- Ability to memorize
- Good penmanship
- An eye for excellence

EQUALS

A study of Ancient Rome using stories to strengthen listening skills, using pictorial narration and short written summaries, thereby facilitating the memorization of people and places and the practice of penmanship, working towards excellence in all they do.

Notice we did not choose government, administration, war, religion, paganism, or the collapse of an empire. Yet we knew what the intent of the study was and could go forward in confidence. Combine knowledge with the skill training your child needs and you will begin to see your semester's emerging style in relation to each child and family's situation. The following table more clearly illustrates this concept.

What the study offers	What we bring to the study	Skill & training needs	Study uniquely suited for each
• Who, what, when, where • Effects of beliefs on culture • Arts & architecture	• Artistic ability • Unstructured teaching style • Interest in stories • Listening skills • Need for small pocket learning	• Narration • Memorization • Good penmanship • Eye for excellence	A study of Ancient Rome using stories to strengthen listening skills, using pictorial narration & short written summaries, facilitating the memorization of people & place & the practice of penmanship striving for excellence in all that was done.

We have done many studies using this method of planning and each one has been a little different from the others. When we studied Ancient Rome there was a lot of reading. Since the people and stories were so intertwined, and my children fairly young, I had them do a picture narration for every day's reading. This accomplished two things, one it gave them something to do while listening, secondly it helped all of us keep straight the characters and flow of stories.

When the children grew and we did science units together, I assigned the older ones individual units of study while the younger still studied the same things. In another history unit I gave my children the choice of narration in any of five ways; either orally, written, pictorially, through poetry or drama. This provided each child the opportunity to choose what they enjoyed most and to excel in that. Other studies I used specifically for the purposes of teaching drama, writing, poetry, and oral or hands-on presentations.

This is just a smattering of the different ways in which a unit of study takes on its own personality. You do not have to determine the style of your semester in Step One, merely keep an eye open for the direction your resources may take you as you walk through the next few steps. Here is an example of how this step could work with different ages of children and a different topic.

World ecosystems and what the study offers	What we bring to the study (styles, responsibility levels & unique needs)	Skills we need to learn (What skills do I need to train?)	Synopsis of the purposes & goals of the semester
• Information about each climate zone in the world • Introduction to ecology • Vocabulary • Geography • How climate affects culture	• Love of books & stories • Interest in art • Knowledge of writing reports • Interest in maps • Need a study that can adapt to five grades • Need time to focus on personal life skills for all	Younger: • Sketching • Comfort with quiet • Responsible self care Middle: • Good penmanship • Following directions • Reading to learn Older: • Critical thinking • Life skills • Study skills All: • Vocabulary development	• Introducing ecosystems • Younger: focus on climate & geography • Older: use critical thinking skills to assess how climate affects culture • Take advantage of new vocabulary making sure to utilize in writing • Review basic writing styles • Encourage independence in older, helping the middle, using narration with the younger

62

It is especially important to take your time during this pre-planning stage. Sufficient time allows for life to happen during the planning process. Generally allow as much time to plan as your intended semester. For instance if you are planning a six-week unit take six weeks to plan. When you are in the thick of "doing" what's already been planned you can spend the time, energy, and brain-power needed to plan what's next.

This does not mean you are going to work every day for weeks planning your next unit or semester. The beauty of this system is that you can work it one step at a time, put it away then pick it up later and still know what to do next. The job of organizing a period of study does not have to be done all in one sitting, or even one weekend. Creative planning can happen when sufficient time is given to think about a semester's emerging style and your family's unique response to it.

Chapter Twelve
Step Two: Brainstorming and Detailing

Step Two is for fleshing out the thinking process. In Step Two you will be making rough notes of all the books, curriculum and other resources you want to use during your next semester. Through the process of becoming familiar with the material available you will end up with the big picture. This overview will allow you to determine what "personality" your semester will have. Look at your chosen resources and consider what schooling style might fit best. Begin to determine what your goals are for this semester. Evaluate which skills might best be taught through the semester. Always keep in mind your family's needs and realities of life. Decide if you are going to do one main unit study and incorporate everything around that or consider whether you will teach some subjects individually. A middle ground approach can be taken; having cohesiveness between some topics while implementing other resources which stand alone, for instance a math textbook or a music theory workbook.

In Step Two we will:
• begin the thinking process
• make rough notes of all books, curriculum and other resources you may want to use
• become familiar with the materials available
• end up with a big picture view of your semester
• decide if you are going to do one main unit study and incorporate everything around that
• decide which subjects need to stand alone
• take sufficient time to plan your semester
• do any necessary pre-reading

As you plan keep in mind your goals for your semester,
your family's needs and realities of life,
and the skills you want to train.

Brainstorming
Brainstorming will encompass two avenues of learning, one being books, curriculum and other paper-based resources that may go with your intended unit of study. Secondly, those activities and field trips that you might like to include.

Paper-Based Resources
Resources in paper form provide tangible ways of assessing the plans of the educator. For this we are largely dependent upon what we receive from others in the form of books, periodicals, and pre-made curriculum. Paper-based resources also enable you to leave a paper trail. Education is not necessarily dependent upon a paper trail and yet for accountability purposes it is often necessary.

Here is what to do as you assess what paper-based resources you may already have in addition to what is available from other sources.

- Read through home school catalogues, visit libraries
- Check out others' resources, browse through your own books
- Identify holes in your resources which will define your shopping list
- Borrow resources from family and friends
- Search for supporting curriculum (eg: worksheets, coloring pages, models, kits, recipes)
- Check out web-based curriculum and worksheet sites

Paper-Based Brainstorming Example:

World Ecosystems

Supportive Literature

My Side of the Mountain
Swiss Family Robinson
Considering God's Creation
Usborne's *World Geography Encyclopedia*
Eyewitness Arctic & Antarctica
The Cranky Blue Crab
The Secret Garden
It Couldn't Just Happen
Science Nature—Mountains & Valleys
Dance in the Desert
The Deer in the Wood
Where the River Begins
Antarctica

Supportive Resource Books

The Usborne Illustrated Thesaurus
Nature Crafts for Kids
Science Crafts for Kids
How Science Works
How Weather Works
I Can Draw Animals
What Shall I Draw Today?
Drawing with Children
The World of Robert Batemen
Mt. St. Helens movie
Finding Out About Deserts
Usborne's *Great Wildlife Search*
First Book of Nature
The Wildlife Year
When I was Young in the Mountains

Brainstorm-Related Activities

Take time to come up with any field trip type ideas related to your study focus. It doesn't matter if you think they will work for your family. Remember you are not committing to anything at this stage, just exploring possibilities. As you compile your list, be sure to leave space for the detailing to come.

- *List activities related to your chosen topic*
- *Explore the possibilities*
- *This is not the place for hands-on craft or science-type projects that will come later*
- *As you make your list, leave space for the detailing to come*

Detailing Activities

Next gather information regarding each idea. Spend time collecting details such as phoning for addresses, determining the cost, times of operation, etc. for each idea. Ask about age appropriateness, stroller friendliness, and any other issues that reflect your realities. Make sure to record phone numbers and email addresses so that you don't have to look them up again. After getting as much information as possible you are in a position to make informed decisions. In the end you may find you only use one idea. However this is one more than if you had not done this step at all. And it just may be the highlight of the semester for you and your family. There is a reproducible form for this in the appendix.

• *Gather information about each idea.*

• *Include details such as phone numbers, web sites, addresses, cost, and times of operation.*

• *Inquire about age appropriateness, stroller friendliness and any other concerns.*

• *After compiling information you will be in a position to make informed decisions.*

Detailing Example:

World Ecosystems

Bloedel Conservatory
@33rd & Cambie St. Vancouver; 604.257.8584; family rate-$1.99/person, 7 people × $1.99 = $13.93; Mon.-Fri. 9 a.m.-8 p.m. Sat. & Sun. 10 a.m.-9 p.m.; invite Grandpa along, go early & be back before rush hour

Green Timbers Park
Go anytime-walk and make a day of it

Greater Vancouver Zoo-www.greatervancouverzoo.com
5048-264 St. Aldergrove; Open 9 a.m.-dusk; family 2 adult + 2 children = $40.00, additional children $9.00 each, so $40.00 + 3 × $9.00 = $67.00 -or- family yearly membership (2 adults + 2 children) / $150.00 + additional children @ $7.00 each = $171.00

Burns Bog
604.572.0373, go anytime, open dawn to dusk, have wooden walkways & possible worksheets from the internet. Take the #640 bus from Scott Rd. Station to sidetrack pub on River Road, follow GVRD access across road south into bog. Bus fare $1.50/child, $2.25/adult, 5 × $1.50 + $2.25 = $9.75. Double that in order to get home, or have dad pick us up on the way home from work, or invite Grandpa for the day and go for free.

Aquarium
604.659.3473; www.vanaqua.org; adults/$14.95, youth 13-28/$11.95, children 4-12/$8.95, parking $3.00/day, so....1 adult ($14.95) + 1 youth ($11.95) + 4 children ($35.80) = $62.70 -or family yearly membership $89.00 + 2 additional children @ $8.95 each = $106.90

Tynehead Nature Park
Anytime-open dawn to dusk

Mount Seymour
Anytime-hike with Grandpa, or possibly Saturday with dad, pack lunch and make a day of it. Depending on weather check the tobogganing or snowshoeing rates.

Beach
Anytime-check tide levels and weather forecast, don't forget buckets and bags for "treasures", pack lunches

---

Chapter Thirteen
Step Three: Categorizing Resources

Step Three is for categorizing your chosen resources and activities from Step Two. This provides you with a visual picture of what you have and what may be needed. At a glance you can see where you may have an imbalance of materials, necessitating the deleting of some materials or the purchasing of others. The following is a sample of a semester's resources for older and younger students.

World Ecosystems

Resources	Older	Younger
Literature	My Side of the Mountain Antarctica Famous Explorers The Yearling	The Secret Garden A House for Hermit Crab Dance in the Desert Lost in the Fog The Cranky Blue Crab The Deer in the Wood Where the River Begins At the End of the Garden
Reference Resources	Usborne's Encyclopedia of World Geography Science Nature-Mountains & Valleys, Usborne's Thesaurus	
	It Couldn't Just Happen	Finding out About Deserts First Book of Nature Great Wildlife Search
Experiments & Crafts	How Science Works How Nature Works How Weather Works	Nature Crafts for Kids Science Crafts for Kids
Book Work (worksheets/coloring)		Considering God's Creation
Field Trips	Planetarium/Aquarium/Tynehead Park/Beach/Burns Bog	
Art, Artists, Poetry	The World of Robert Bateman	
	Drawing with Children	I Can Draw Animals What Shall I Draw Today?
Videos	Mount St. Helens Video & Mount Everest Video	
Miscellaneous	Excellence in Writing Curriculum	
Other		Play-dough

At a glance this form looks well filled out with varying options for both the older and the younger students. The thing is that depending on how long the semester is going to be there just may be too much material here. So it will be important in the following steps to think critically about the work load represented in this table.

It is quite possible to have three books that would take the same amount of time and energy as one larger book. It is also possible to have a larger resource book that is only used sparingly and that would take little time and energy as compared to three smaller books. So it is not only important to assess the number of materials but also the educational volume of the materials at your disposal.

Into this equation is the skill set you are bringing to the study in addition to what your educational goals are through the study. Two different children, both the same ages, but at different levels of reading or writing would demand that these same resources be used in different ways.

And here it is wise take into account your family's realities and individual limitations, determining what exact work load would be feasible for you and your children at this time. In this way begin thinking about your children and how they would best benefit from the materials at hand, tucking the information away to be pulled out as the process of making a semester's study unfolds.

Chapter Fourteen
Step Four: Semester Length and Outline

By now you should have a fairly good idea of how much material you plan to use for your semester. It is now time to determine how many weeks it will take to utilize your chosen resources. Think about how often you want to study; twice a week perhaps for kindergartners, or up to five days a week for older students. Does it look like you have more reading or more hands-on material for this semester? Is the material you found best taught in large portions of time or bit by bit? For example, hands-on science needs larger chunks of time, perhaps once or twice a week, whereas historical novels more often are best done a chapter at a time. Check to see how many weeks you have until major holidays, trips, planned breaks, and such.

It is also important to consider the time of the year and the type of study. It has never worked in our home to do history units in the summer. It is much nicer doing all that reading snuggled up on a couch during the winter. It is also a very good idea not to schedule every week that you have available. Leave a week or perhaps a day of the week for catch-up. This leaves a bit of space for the unpredictable to happen in the midst of children and home.

Determine the length of your semester:
• by how much material you plan to use
• by how many weeks it will take to utilize your chosen resources
• by considering the time of year and type of study
• by checking how many weeks are available to you
• by leaving margin for the unpredictable

Example: *World Ecosystems/Twelve-Week Fall Study*

SEPTEMBER						
Sunday	Monday	Tuesday	Wednesday	Thursday	Friday	Saturday
1	2 Labor Day	3	4	5	6	7
			Week One			
8	9	10	11	12	13	14
			Week Two			
15	16	17	18	19	20	21
			Week Three			
22	23	24	25	26	27 *B-day*	28
			Week Four			
29	30					

OCTOBER

Sunday	Monday	Tuesday	Wednesday	Thursday	Friday	Saturday
		1	2	3	4	5 *Ladies Retreat*
	Week Five (Mon–Fri)					
6	7	8	9	10	11 *Anniversary*	12
	Week Six (Mon–Fri)					
13	14 Canadian Thanksgiving	15	16	17	18	19
	Week Seven (Mon–Fri)					
20	21	22	23	24	25 *B-day*	26 *B-day*
	Week Eight (Mon–Fri)					
27	28	29	30	31		
	Week Nine (Mon–Fri)					

NOVEMBER

Sunday	Monday	Tuesday	Wednesday	Thursday	Friday	Saturday
					1	2
3	4	5	6	7	8	9
	Week Ten (Mon–Fri)					
10	11 Remembrance Day	12	13	14	15	16
	Week Eleven (Mon–Fri)					
17	18	19 *B-day*	20	21	22	23
	Week Twelve (Mon–Fri)					
24	25	26	27	28 U.S. Thanksgiving	29	30

Can you see why it is important to overview the length of your semester, taking the time to put in holidays, birthdays, and such? I don't know about you but I need an extra day to think about birthdays, taking the time and mental energy required to make it a special day. And if I didn't pre-see the holidays coming I would plan a day's worth of work and then get there and find myself out of sync with what I'd planned and what life was presenting.

If there is going to be a four-day study week, it is good to know at the beginning and plan accordingly. This step doesn't take much time and there are some calendar blanks in the appendix to help you out.

Next you will see how to give a focus to each week of your semester.

Determining a Semester's Outline

The most important thing to determine is what will be the skeleton or framework of your study. Choose a book or a study focus (such as drama, art or poetry) to be the skeleton of your study. Following are some examples of the different approaches by which to outline a semester based on the resources you wish to use.

Reference Book (needs good overview without excessive detail)

Choose a book which gives a good overview without too much detail. Often the table of contents can become the framework by assigning each chapter its own week or even month. Detailing then comes from other resources. Every other book or activity can then be placed into where it fits best.

For instance, when we studied Ancient Greece I had two main reference books I used. *Ancient Greece*, by Eyewitness Books, with fifteen two-page spreads; each double page picture had a paragraph summarizing the topic. My other reference was *Usborne's Ancient Greece*. Usborne books have a plethora of information and sub-topics; too much to be the skeleton of a study. It therefore quite naturally worked to make the Eyewitness book the skeleton of our unit, assigning each two-page spread its own week, then delegating the Usborne information into the appropriate week.

- *Table of contents can often become your framework*
- *You might assign each chapter its own week*
- *Detailing comes from other sources*

Curriculum

There are many excellent curriculums out there for every subject imaginable. And it makes a lot of sense to organize how you will use those curriculums in a semester along with the other options you have chosen. A curriculum is often a skeleton all its own around which other books and projects become accessories.

- *Determine how many pages you want to accomplish in the desired time*
- *Each week ends up with its own theme*
- *Round out the curriculum with other resources*

Literature

This can also work with literature although in a slightly different way. Each chapter would need to be pre-read to determine what would best be taught from it. Then assign reference information appropriately. For instance, if the book *Swallows and Amazons* was our skeleton, while reading the first chapter we could cover boating terminology. During the second chapter wilderness camping could be covered. The third chapter would be ideal for studying letter writing or geographical terms such as cove, harbor, inlets, etc. This idea would be continued with each chapter. It is particularly nice to do this if you have a book that you love and wish to use it in depth.

- *Pre-read the book*
- *Determine what could best be taught from each chapter*

• These become your weekly focuses
• Additional materials can be used to round out each week's focus

Study Focus (e.g.: drama, art, poetry)

When making drama the study focus find a good resource book to become your outline and then tie it into your accompanying study of history, or in the case of younger children make a play out of any book that you are reading.

Example: Drama
- Think: what do we want to learn about drama? (Do we need to do drama? read drama? technical side? famous actors and actresses? historical drama?)
- Determine the specific focus.
- Determine the sub-steps to learning the specific focus.
- These sub-steps become your framework.

These are a few of the numerous ways to create a skeleton of what you desire to study. Once you have decided on your skeleton construct your outline at a glance. In the following examples I used the book Usborne's *Encyclopedia of World Geography*, taking a section heading as my rough outline.

Having an outline of your semester at a glance gives a fantastic at a glance picture of your basic lesson plan. And it is very helpful if you are accountable to your local school district and need to show them what your educational plans are for the semester or year. It also keeps yourself focused on what "this" week is about as you get there. Following is an example of a combined Semester and Focus Outline at a glance.

World Ecosystems Outline

Week	Date	Topic
One	Sept. 3–6	Plant Life on Earth
Two	Sept. 9–13	Animal Life on Earth
Three	Sept. 16–20	Ecosystems
Four	Sept. 23–27	People & Ecosystems
Five	Sept. 30–Oct. 3	Rainforests
Six	Oct. 7–11	Tropical Grasslands
Seven	Oct. 15–18	Monsoons
Eight	Oct. 21–25	Tropical Deserts
Nine	Oct. 28–Nov. 1	Mediterranean Climates
Ten	Nov. 4–8	Temperate Climates
Eleven	Nov. 12–15	Polar Regions
Twelve	Nov. 18–22	Mountains

SEPTEMBER

Sunday	Monday	Tuesday	Wednesday	Thursday	Friday	Saturday
1	2 Labor Day	3	4	5	6	7
		Week One: Plant Life on Planet Earth				
8	9	10	11	12	13	14
		Week Two: Animal Life on Earth				
15	16	17	18	19	20	21
		Week Three: Ecosystems				
22	23	24	25	26	27 *B-day*	28
		Week Four: People and Ecosystems				
29	30					

OCTOBER

Sunday	Monday	Tuesday	Wednesday	Thursday	Friday	Saturday
		1	2	3	4	5
		Week Five: Rainforests			*Ladies Retreat*	
6	7	8	9	10	11 *Anniversary*	12
		Week Six: Tropical Grasslands				
13	14 Canadian Thanksgiving	15	16	17	18	19
		Week Seven: Monsoons				
20	21	22	23	24	25 *B-day*	26 *B-day*
		Week Eight: Tropical Deserts				
27	28	29	30	31		
		Week Nine: Mediterranean Climates				

NOVEMBER

Sunday	Monday	Tuesday	Wednesday	Thursday	Friday	Saturday
					1	2
3	4	5	6	7	8	9
		Week Ten: Temperate Climates				
10	11 Remembrance Day	12	13	14	15	16
		Week Eleven: Polar Regions				
17	18	19 *B-day*	20	21	22	23
		Week Twelve: Mountains				
24	25	26	27	28 U.S. Thanksgiving	29	30

Chapter Fifteen
Step Five: Weekly Outline

Now we will begin to outline our weekly goals. To begin with you will need a "Weekly Outline Form" for every week of your study; you will find a reproducible form for this in the appendix. I like to lay them all out on my dining room table. I then label each with the topic, proposed week and sub-topic for that week as decided in Step Four.

Now refer back to Step Three's list of categorized resources and one category at a time put the resources into the weeks where they fit best. I find it time efficient to fill the same category for every week before going onto another category. For instance I would fill in all of the writing assignment spaces before going onto another category.

Or you can choose to take a book and extract everything out of it and into the best categories before going onto another book. For instance, if I had an Eyewitness Boats book I would look at every page and put each into the week in which it best fits. I would then take another book and insert its parts into the appropriate weeks.

A pencil is suggested, or sticky notes, as it is not uncommon for things to get changed around in the process. Here is a sampling of a weekly outline.

Weekly Outline: World Ecosystems
Focus: Plant Life on Earth
Week: One

Component	Older	Younger
Reading	_Encyclopedia of World Geography_, pg. 108 _How Science Works_, pg. 136: "Climate Distribution & Vegetation" Begin reading _The Yearling_	_First Book of Nature_: "Trees", pg. 25-48 Begin reading _My Side of the Mountain_ (22 chapters=1/day including weekends)
Worksheets	Make a map of the world's climate zones as found on pg. 136 in _How Science Works_	"Tree Detective" & "Portrait of a Tree" pages from _Considering God's Creation_ picture puzzle from _First Book of Nature_
Language Study	Advanced dress-ups, dual adverbs, verbs or adjectives, from _Excellence in Writing_	Vivid word list, nouns and pronouns from _Excellence in Writing_
Writing Assignments	Week's Task: Notes and summary. All of pgs. 108-109 except the blue squared paragraph in _World Geography_	Week's Task: Notes and summary from pg. 109 in _World Geography_ "Why do we need plants?"

continued

Component	Older	Younger
Hands-on	*How Nature Works* Pg. 57 "Measuring the Height of a Tree"	*Nature Crafts for Kids* "Bark Rubbing" pg. 134 "Leaf Prints" pg. 56
Art/Artists/ Poetry	*The World of Robert Bateman* pg. 8 make your own copy of Bateman's picture	*What Shall I Draw Today?* Pg. 7 *At the End of the Garden* Pg. 41 (poem)
Field Trip/ Video/Misc.	Walk at Tynehead	
Other	Begin working through the book *Homework on Your Computer*	

How to Use Your Weekly Outline

Reading
  • Reading assignments for the week

Worksheets
  • List worksheets here
  • Include worksheet address
  • On sticky note list photocopying needs

Language Study
  • Put teaching goal to the left
  • Don't break the goal down here; that is for step six

Writing Assignments
  • You may desire to follow writing curriculum
  • Put goal to the left
  • Include particulars of where to find teacher helps

Hands-on
  • Put titles, book and page number of interactive activities
  • Use a sticky note to state any needed supplies or materials

Art/Artists/Poetry
  • List books and page number of resources
  • List titles and page numbers of desired projects
  • Use sticky notes to generate shopping list

Field Trip/Video/Miscellaneous
  • List all applicable information
  • Put directions on a sticky note

Other
  • Whatever you want that I've not included—perhaps math pages or piano practice
  • Great place to include ideas for the little ones

Chapter Sixteen
Step Six: Daily Outline

Step Six takes your goals from the weekly outline and organizes the information day by day, breaking down each goal into mini goals. Step Six is not necessary if you want to work task to task throughout the week. In fact, unless you are a very structured person with structured children, I recommend you skip this step. The exception would be during seasons of extreme stress or crisis. During our stressful periods I found it very difficult to home school without a daily to-do list. Step Six gives you a checklist for those seasons.

• *This step is for taking your weekly outline and organizing the information day by day.*
• *The goal is to have each weekly objective from Step Five broken down into mini tasks.*
• *There are two forms for this step: one for older children and one for kindergarten through grade three.*

Again mark any doctor appointments, field trips, and holidays first as these things will affect what can be accomplished in a day. Choose a category and fill it out for every week before moving onto another. There are two reproducible forms in the appendix, one for older children, and the other for kindergarten through third grade.

How to Use Your Daily Outline

Component	Monday	Tuesday	Wednesday	Thursday	Friday
Reading	Reading assignments can be for your children to read or for you to read to your children. The information for this section comes from your Step Three's list of literature or reference resources. Here is where you break it down into specifics. If you have children old enough for reading assignments but not quite ready for a full assignment page (step seven) consider writing the assignment in colored ink. This facilitates the child being able to see at a glance what they need to be reading.				
Work-sheets	Obviously this is the place to list any worksheets that you have. More than anything it becomes a reminder to you that you have worksheets to go with your study. It ensures that your efforts to make or find worksheets do not go to waste.				
Language Study	I use this space for what I specifically want to teach my children. This section may strongly correlate with the writing assignment section. Or it may concentrate more on grammar, phonics, or specific writing styles. It may also overlap with the worksheets section, your part in the teaching of it to be written here. The goal for the week can be written to the left while each day is assigned the specified task needed in order to accomplish the goal.				
Vocabulary & Spelling	This section can be used in a number of ways. It can be used to merely map out what pages are expected to be done in a spelling or vocabulary book. You can list the spelling words you are going to teach and test your children on. Or you can make reference to the paragraph or poem to use for dictation and spelling.				

continued

Component	Monday	Tuesday	Wednesday	Thursday	Friday
Writing Assignments	I use my writing curriculum for my guide regarding what to teach next. I put the week's goal to the left as well as what page or section of my writing curriculum it is found in. Then I break up the task into bite-sized pieces for the week. For instance, if I want to teach my children the process for a simple essay, I would put Simple Essay; section VIII to the left. For each day I would then specify the task, Monday: teach outline and brainstorm topics; Tuesday: research three sources; Wednesday: make notes and write first draft; Thursday: edit; Friday: write good copy.				
Hands-on	The fun stuff goes here such as collages, models made from clay or wood, science experiments, as well as anything you might want to do.				
Art/ Artists/ Poetry	Study famous pictures that deal with the same subject matter as your unit. Or find a good reference book on how to draw, then use your own sub-topics to practice new and review techniques.				
Field Trip/ Video/ Misc.	This section is quite self explanatory. It is handy to put instructions about a field trip on a sticky note, then when it's time to go the information is handy.				
Other	This section is for whatever you want that doesn't really fit into any other category. It may be math, science text, a second language, physical education, home economics, woodworking, Bible, or manners of the week. It is also an ideal place to specify ideas for the little tykes who don't "do school" yet need something to occupy them.				

Reading
- Provides space to specify each day's reading versus the week's reading
- You may want to consider putting reading assignments in colored ink

Worksheets
- Provides space to specify which day you want to use available worksheets and where to find them

Language Study
- This section is for what I want to teach
- The goal for the week can be written to the left
- Each day's specific task can be assigned as needed in order to accomplish the week's goal

Vocabulary/Spelling
- Can be used to map out what pages of a spelling or vocabulary workbook are expected to be done
- Include particulars of where to find teacher helps for each day as needed
- Make reference to the paragraph or poem to use for dictation

Writing Assignments
- You may want to use writing curriculum to guide your goals
- Put the week's goal to the left along with where to find the particulars, then break up the task into bite-sized pieces for the week

Hands-On
- Same as the weekly outline, except this form provides space to block off time in the week. In this way you can make sure that you are not filling each day's schedule too full

Art/Artists/Poetry
- Same as the weekly outline yet provides opportunity to assign your goal to a specific day of the week.
- List famous pictures that relate to your study
- Use reference book about drawing and make each week a new focus, practicing and reviewing techniques

Field Trip/Video/Miscellaneous
- Same as weekly outline, just apply what you plan to do to a specific day or days

Other
- Again, apply your weekly goals to a specific day of the week

Daily Outline for Younger Children

In the early years home schooling needs differ from the middle or later years. Again, empty spaces are not negative, they merely reflect the choices you have made for yourself and your children at this time in your lives.

How to Use Your K-3 Daily Outline

Component	Monday	Tuesday	Wednesday	Thursday	Friday
Language Study	Included in this section would be the technical stuff such as phonics or spelling. It could also include specifics like poetry, writing styles, plays or anything else you personally desire to use it for.				
Read Aloud	Read aloud can be intended for your child, yourself, or for both of you. Use this space to either pre-think and determine what you are going to read or as a place to record what has been read.				
Worksheet	If you have specific worksheets to go with your focus of study this is the place to list them. I wouldn't bother listing the pages of a workbook as these are usually worked page by page from day to day. Although if you desire to skip around in a workbook this is the place to specify which pages.				
Science/ Socials	I've put science and socials together because in the early grades most home schoolers don't try to do both science and social separately every day of the week.				

continued

Component	Monday	Tuesday	Wednesday	Thursday	Friday
Math	This is for mom to know what she needs to be teaching in math as well as what the child's reinforcement exercises are. The goal for the week could be written to the left. Then break the goal into bite-sized tasks to ensure that the goal is accomplished.				
Art	For the sake of clarity let's define art as drawing and painting. I realize that hands-on activities can and should be considered art. Yet the purpose of doing an outline is to have a reminder of what we desire our children to learn, and us to teach. So here put the week's art goal, or restate the month's goal at the left and then you can break the goal into bite-sized tasks for as many days per week as you desire.				
Hands-on	Activities for this section would include anything from paper crafts to elaborate collages out of ceramic tiles or rocks. Pre-planning will enable you to make sure you have the materials needed. It is especially handy to put what you don't have onto a small sticky note on the appropriate week. This way, when you scan through the weeks you can see what is still required and take the sticky note with you shopping.				
Field Trip	Whatever field trips you plan make sure to put all the information down, including any phone numbers needed. Put addresses onto sticky notes, then when the day comes you can transfer it to your vehicle or purse and you are ready to go.				
Misc.	This could be the place to put down your own to do list, or maybe meal plans, for the week. Then everything is in one place. Otherwise use it for whatever you have that I've not mentioned.				
Other	Here is a good spot to write ideas for your younger children who do not have any "school" yet need to be occupied.				

Remember

Language Study
- List technical studies such as phonics, spelling, etc.
- Could include specifics such as poetry, writing styles, etc.

Read Aloud
- Read aloud intended for your child or yourself
- Use this space to pre-think and plan what to read, or to record what has been read

Worksheet
- This is useful if you desire to skip around in a workbook
- List corresponding worksheets and any photocopying needs

Science/Socials
  • List the focus and goals of each day you choose to study this in a week's time

Math
  • List teacher helps and addresses
  • Write intended goals or record what was accomplished

Art
  • Defined as drawing and painting
  • State what your children are to learn and you to teach

Hands-On
  • Activities for this section include paper crafts
  • Pre-planning enables the acquisition of all needed materials in a timely manner
  • Put what is needed on sticky notes for your errand day

Field Trip
  • This is the place for all pertinent information (use sticky notes to go)

Miscellaneous
  • This is for anything else you might want to add

Other
  • List ideas for younger children who don't do "school" yet need to be occupied

Chapter Seventeen
Step Seven: Assignment Sheet

Once your child is reading you can take the weekly and daily outlines and turn them into weekly assignment sheets.

My older children really like this and it is a simple way to give responsibility with appropriate authority. I tell them that it doesn't matter to me what order, and sometimes even when, they do the work just so that it is done by the end of the week. We try to incorporate some sort of reward gained or privilege lost at the end of the week by way of motivation. Yet I have found that just being able to be their own boss and knowing what is expected is often motivation enough.

Changing Roles

It is hardly necessary to explain the benefits for both the mother and child of doing this. The child learns time management, self-discipline and educational consequences. Mom is relieved of motivating and/or supervising her child.

The assignment sheet becomes the facilitator thus allowing mom to put her energies into mothering more than teaching. Occasionally too, the assignment sheet can be the bearer of bad news (an unpleasant task), distancing mom a bit from the negative emotion.

As my children stepped into the teenage years assignment sheets became especially necessary because at this stage they really wanted me to listen to them and dialogue about life in general. In the pre-teen and teen years I have found it crucial that I manage our home-schooling in a way which allows for me to be mentally and emotionally available to them as mom more than teacher.

Assigning Responsibility

In the younger years it was my responsibility to teach my children, to be their driving force and to set in place good study habits. Good study habits can be defined as following directions, being consistent, and sticking with a task even though it is not liked or is difficult. In the early years it is most often moms who ensure that learning becomes this. In fact is it not often mom learning the very same things? Yet as children mature, if mom continues to be the driving force we actually hinder the learning of good study habits. If we continue to be the one that forces this into the teen years, then what has the child really learned in the long run but to only work when mom is around?

I have found that when I take on the responsibility of making sure my older children get their school work done I am greatly hindered in fulfilling my own responsibilities toward my younger children and my home. It comes down to boundaries—what is my responsibility and what is my child's responsibility? Learning needs to gradually become the responsibility of the child.

Breaking it Down

It is through weekly assignment sheets that I have been able to pass the baton of responsibility of learning to my child. The key to creating successful assignment sheets is breaking the tasks down into very simple steps; the younger the child the simpler the steps. This ensures that there is no misunderstanding as to what is expected. I have found this really helps me to fully think through and relay to my children what I expect from them. Too often I have been vague in relaying my expectations, resulting in frustration for all of us.

The Benefits

- Children are motivated by knowing what is expected.
- Children learn time management, self-discipline and educational consequences.
- Assignment sheets take the pressure off mom so she can put her energies into mothering more than teaching.
- Mom is relieved from having to remember where multiple children are in their studies.
- Learning becomes the responsibility of the child.
- Breaking tasks down into simple steps helps mom fully think through and relay to students what is expected of them.
- Life gains balance.
- Home schooling is more manageable and enjoyable.

How to Tell Whether It's Working

A simple way to assess if your assignment sheets are appropriate for your child is to see how much of it they can accomplish on their own.

Obviously when they are young the main goals are to teach each child the skills of following a to-do list and to take initiative for their learning even if that means coming to mom for help. But I want my older children to be able to study on their own at least 50 to 75 percent of the time.

If my student is not capable of completing upwards of three-quarters of his assignments without me then I have obviously made the assignments too difficult. If the assignments are too difficult to complete independently then my assignment sheet is not accomplishing what I intended it to do. My child is not coming away with a sense of success and my time is not freed up to attend to my own daily responsibilities which may include the teaching of younger children.

Assessing Your Assignment Sheet

- *How much can my child accomplish on his own?*
- *An older child should be able to do 50 to 75 percent of their studying on their own.*
- *If my grade five student cannot complete half of his work, then the assignments are too difficult.*
- *Is my child coming away with a sense of accomplishment?*
- *Is my time freed up to attend to my own daily responsibilities?*

Sample of Older Student's Weekly Assignments

Week One
World Ecosystems: Plant Life on Earth

· Read pages 108 & 109 in the <u>Encyclopedia of World Geography</u>

· Read page 136 " Climate Distribution & Vegetation" in <u>How Science Works</u>

· Begin reading <u>The Yearling</u>; must read at least one chapter per day

· Make a replica of the "climate zones map" as shown on page 136 in <u>How Science Works</u>

· This week's writing task, "Notes & Summary"
   – take notes from <u>World Geography</u> reading assignment
   – do a written summary of your notes
   – incorporate into your writing 'dual adverbs, verbs & adjectives' as taught by mom
   – edit: check spelling, punctuation & grammar
   – write good copy

· Look at page 8 in <u>The World of Robert Bateman</u>

· Mom has spelling words for you on Monday
   – Study spelling words during the week
   – Take spelling test on Friday

· This week's outing is a walk at Tynehead on Thursday
   – Take your sketchbook and do some sketches of different foliage
   – Do "Measuring the Height of a Tree", pg.57 from <u>How Nature Works</u>, read before going and either take notes about how or take book with
   – Collect leaves and flowers for drying
   – Press your leaves and flowers once home

· Math: four lessons this week
   – lesson one
   – lesson two
   – lesson three
   – lesson four

· Chores
   –Monday
   –Tuesday
   –Wednesday
   –Thursday
   –Friday

[Here is where I would put extra stuff, such as music practice, extracurricular lessons or tutoring (especially if there is homework to be remembered), as well as special projects such as <u>Homework on Your Computer</u>.]

Younger Student's Weekly Assignments Sample

Week One
World Ecosystems: Plant Life on Earth

- With Mom read pages 108 & 109 in the *Encyclopedia of World Geography*

- Listen to Mom read *My Side of the Mountain* (one chapter per day)

- Read pages 25-48, "Trees," in first *Book of Nature* by the end of the week

- Do a "picture puzzle" that Mom has for you

- This week's writing task, "Notes & Summary"
    - Read the blue section from page 109 in *Encyclopedia of World Geography*
    - Make notes from each sentence
    - Do an oral summary or speech of your notes for Mom
    - Do a written summary of your notes
    - Add in any dress-ups that you know
    - With mom learn about vivid nouns and pronouns and add them to your paragraph
    - Edit
        - check spelling
        - check pronunciation
        - check grammar
    - Write good copy of your paragraph

- Mom has spelling words for you on Monday
    - Study spelling words during the week
    - Take spelling test on Friday

- This week's outing is a walk at Tynehead on Thursday
    - Take your sketchbook and do some sketches of different foliage
    - Take "tree detective" and "portrait of a tree" pages with and enter information about trees you see
    - Take some paper out of your sketchbook and do some bark rubbing and leaf prints
    - Collect some leaves and flowers to dry at home
    - Press your leaves and flowers once home

- Draw from the lesson on page 7 in *What Shall I Draw Today?*

- Look at page 8 in *The World of Robert Bateman*

- Read the poem on page 41 in *At the End of the Garden*

- Math: four lessons this week
    1st lesson   2nd lesson   3rd lesson   4th lesson

- Chores:
    Monday   Tuesday   Wednesday   Thursday   Friday

[Here is where I would put extra stuff such as music practice.]

The Assignment Sheet as a Tool

An assignment sheet is not going to be the one "thing" which makes your home schooling perfect. But it is a very powerful tool that I trust will make your home schooling more manageable and enjoyable.

The structure assignment sheets provide can offer a powerful amount of freedom when there are times Mom needs to be away for a planned absence, or an unexpected one. Perhaps a baby is due (You've plenty of time to prepare for that!), but should baby come early the assignments are in place and school can go on if for instance Grandma has come to help.

Assignment sheets could even facilitate a day or partial day off for Mom when the kids are older.

Planning that Provides Options

More than anything I have found assignment sheets give balance to life, enabling us to be responsible to all of life, and enabling us to enjoy life as well.

Numerous times my children have been up early getting as much done as possible so that they can take full advantage of other opportunities which may come their way later in the day or week; opportunities such as working with Grandpa on church maintenance projects, playing with cousins, or going to work with dad. It frees our family to take advantage of sunny days, (which can be few and far between in the Vancouver area), or of turning my husband's unexpected days off into errand days.

For myself it frees me to be more than a home schooling mom. I am able to be a woman who happens to home school her children. I am able to be wife, mother, a friend with friends, writer, and more. I am able to participate in areas of my spiritual gifting which is a very important part of who God has made me to be. In short, life is able to have balance.

An unbalanced life is a life that burns out. And none of us are home schooling with the goal of burning out. So as you make assignment sheets remember that as with every other step, Step Seven is a tool to use and not to be enslaved to. Leave some margin in your planning; more than anything making it work for you and your family.

Assignment Sheet Variations

I have played around with a number of different variations of the assignment sheets. Full-fledged assignment sheets are very useful at times, yet at other times they are more than what is needed.

And often a combined assignment/checklist is just the thing; providing direction yet taking less time to produce while still keeping track at a glance what is to be and what has been done.

Following is a sample of how to take the semester's outline from Step Four and the resource list from Step Three, combining the rough goals and resources of each into an assignment sheet and checklist for an older student.

Twelve-Week Semester: World Ecosystems

- Choose two of the following books to read, followed by a book report for one of them:
  - _My Side of the Mountain_
  - _Antarctica_
  - _Famous Explorers_
  - _The Yearling_

- Using Usborne's _Encyclopedia of World Geography_ write an essay about world ecosystems and their effects upon mankind.

- Choose either _It Just Couldn't Happen_ or _Science Nature-Mountains & Valleys_, reading, and then preparing a news article about something that struck you as you read.

- Choose four experiments from the following books:
  - _How Science Works_
  - _How Nature Works_
  - _How Weather Works_
  - Take pictures as you proceed; write scientific process notes for one.

- Browse through _The World of Robert Bateman_, choose three pictures and make your own rendition. Use different art mediums for each.

- Watch Mount St. Helens and Mount Everest videos. Practice note-taking with one of them.

- Make a map of the world's climate zones.

- At the planetarium take along a sketchbook and record what you see.

	M	T	W	T	F	M	T	W	T	F	M	T	W	T	F	M	T	W	T	F
Reading																				
Writing																					
Art/ Experiments																					
Math																					
Worldly Wise																					
Grammar																					
Piano																					
Chores																					

Having a checklist is an easy way for me to assess how much the child has done in a day, week, or as we at one time arranged it, in four-week blocks. A checklist removes the pressure of a daily to-do list. To-do lists may take longer than is good for us. As I see it a to-do list is what I want to accomplish within a given period of time whereas a checklist is a guide to what needs to be accomplished giving fluidity as to the particulars of when and how. A checklist removes a sense of being driven. It allows our options to remain fluid and gives opportunity for me to step in and suggest areas that may need particular attention on any given day.

Sometimes a Checklist is Just the Thing

A checklist gives guidance to the children to decide in what order to do their work. I find myself satisfied with what is done during our study hours and while some days I teach and direct other days they freely work from their list. Each day has its own rhythm and a check sheet allows for this.

A checklist does not mean that I don't plan; I need to plan for me. But I usually stop at a weekly outline and then present my children with their own checklist. This works well if I have the brain power and emotional energy to really focus on home schooling for a period of time. If I know there are going to be other life issues that will take a lot of my focus or that will consistently interrupt our study hours then I go back to the full assignment sheet. I also use the full assignment sheets when I am personally losing momentum. That is most often at the end of the school year and sometimes right after Christmas. Otherwise I have found checklists are very adequate and they do not take an extraordinary amount of time to produce.

An effective way to combine check sheets and specific assignments would be to use the check sheets for those subjects which need to remain fluid, like math for instance; as math can mean a game, flash-cards, manipulative play, pages in a textbook, drill (verbally or on paper) or worksheets.

A friend of mine makes her plans and then writes each day's assignments on the white board for her two sons. This allows for a flexible outflow of her plans and she says it does not take too long to write them out. Even when only four of mine needed direction I would not have had neither time nor space to write out everyone's assignments every day. This is a perfect example of how making decisions about the how of home schooling is determined in large part by each family's realities.

Home schooling forever needs adjustment and it will probably remain a reality that what worked last month or last year will not work for the present. This is when variations of assignment sheets can give momentum.

Chapter Eighteen
Keeping it in Balance

John Taylor Gatto in his book *Dumbing Us Down* says:
"The lessons of school prevent children from keeping important appointments with themselves and with their families to learn lessons in self-motivation, perseverance, self-reliance, courage, dignity, and love—and lessons in service to others, too, which are among the key lessons of home and community life."

Many of us educate our children at home for reasons very similar to these. Yet overzealous home schooling families can keep their children so busy that the opportunity to learn the real stuff they need to be learning is missed. I have been one of those moms. The system of management I have just shared with you is potentially dangerous. As with any new tool we are enthusiastic about, it can be overused. I believe that this system is useful for certain seasons of life or situations such as:

- times of extreme busyness, stress or crisis
- times when you want to establish good work habits
- teaching specific study tools, such as how to write a report
- teaching numerous grades at once
- times when your primary focus needs to be on something other than education

Once foundational skills have been taught and good study habits have been established it is a delight to release our children to apply what they've learned to areas of their own interest.

Walnuts of Learning

My grandma had a pint jar containing six walnuts and one cup of rice. The reality of this combination is if you put the rice in before the walnuts, the walnuts will not fit. Yet if the walnuts are put in first, the rice then fits in around the walnuts. My Grandma compared the walnuts to Bible reading and the rice as all the other stuff of life. Sandra Burnett in her book, *Celebrate with Joy*, speaks of the rice as being all that needs to be done at Christmas time while the walnuts represent the truly important things of the Christmas season. In each of these illustrations it becomes clear that if we prioritize the most important the rest will fit in.

Once again I have filtered these analogies through the home schooling sieve. For me the rice represents the technical aspects of education, like spelling, grammar, math and so on. The walnuts represent pieces of real life, such as real responsibilities, real authority, and real privileges. For too many years I, quite conscientiously, filled our home schooling experience with the rice of technicalities. Yet what I dismissed as unimportant were the pieces of life that we desperately needed. So I began working at giving each of our children what I call "pieces of life". For one it has been the ownership of a dog and all the authority, responsibility and privileges that are a part of that. Another had a paper route for a time. And as they've grown there have been bank accounts, debit cards and again, the accompanying authority, responsibility, and privilege.

Walnuts Represent
· pieces of real life
· real responsibilities
· real authority
· real privileges

Rice Represents
· technical aspects of education
· spelling
· grammar
· math

We used to live in a 1200 sq.ft. townhouse with limited yard and virtually no garden. We lived on a very busy street, with any "wild" areas being too dangerous to allow the children to play on their own. At that time it was difficult to come up with pieces of life in the city, yet we persisted in making this a priority for we saw the value of getting those "walnuts" into life, knowing that the "rice" would fit in.

Brainstorm for yourself: *What would pieces of life look like for my children?*

_____

_____

_____

_____

_____

_____

In addition to the pieces of life that must complement the technicalities of education, we also must model to our children life outside of book work. It is as I have pursued interests that my children see that there is a purpose in pursuing that which comprises real life.

Clay and Sally Clarkson, authors of *Educating the WholeHearted Child* call this "discretionary studies", meaning life skills and abilities, natural gifts and community involvement. We want our children to be self-starters, to grow into mature adults, to pursue education, to have a vision for what they can be and do. Yet all too often we find ourselves busy, busy, busy with book work and wonder why we have children who've lost their curiosity about life.

Ask yourself: *With what fruitless activities am I keeping my children busy?*

_____

_____

_____

_____

_____

What fruitful activities am I giving my children access to?

_____

_____

_____

_____

_____

The scale I use to determine if I am going overboard in my planning is by measuring my children's level of curiosity and creativity. When they do not play cooperatively together, don't know what to do, or are not inquiring about life, I know that I have been pushing all of us too hard. There must be time for, as a friend says, "delight learning".

In trying to keep the balance in our own lives I am learning to plan and then to hold my plans with an open hand. Creating objectives and goals is part of my responsibility in teaching, yet what I teach my child is only a portion of their education. According to Gatto that should comprise about 40% of their time, the other 60% being given to what Gatto in *Dumbing us Down* describes as:

"Allowing as many of the kids I taught as possible the raw material people have always used to educate themselves: privacy, choice, freedom from surveillance, and as broad a range of situations and human associations as my limited power and resources could manage."

As I've learned to organize our education I now intuitively know what can be learned from various studies. I recognize the different angles to approach our education. Perhaps it has been because of the writing out of objectives and goals that I find education flows out of who I am—it is no longer a coat I put on. Because of this I can give my children more freedom to learn on their own, for I am more confident in my own ability to respond to their current life season.

Use this system until you don't need it anymore, or you only need a portion of it. In the meantime, find rest in knowing you're covering all the bases.

Chapter Nineteen
Matters of the Heart

When I began home schooling what I heard time and again from those further down the road than I was, "Take 3-5 years to figure out your children's styles and your teaching styles, and how to organize." I naively assumed that once this was figured out the rest would be smooth sailing. This has not been so. I know our family's styles, I know how to organize, and I know how to choose. Yet I have had to come to grips with the reality that my maximum output is not always sufficient for the demand. Learning about and accepting our styles, learning how to organize and choosing well has added stability to our home schooling, but it has not changed the reality that home schooling brings me face to face with my own inadequacies.

As home schooling has brought me face to face with my own inadequacies there have been periods of time when I've felt on the edge of failure in virtually every area of my life. The intensity of home schooling supports the lie that "my best is not good enough." Somewhere along the way I began believing that if I just tried harder, organized more, worked better, that life would be more manageable, better. There is truth in this, yet I have also found another truth to be this, that once I've learned to manage the externals I am suddenly face to face with my own self. And internal heart and character problems are much more difficult and painful to confront.

Facing Inadequacies

So what do we do when faced with our own inadequacies? I suggest that we first of all come to terms, as I've mentioned before, with who we are, what we value, what we are about. We need to understand our strengths and weaknesses. We need to give ourselves permission to be real and to be authentic. It is only in authenticity that we clearly face ourselves and ultimately mature. If I know who I am and what I am to be about, I can then filter the bombardment of expectations from myself, my spouse, my children, friends, family, and on and on.

As home schoolers so much of our time and energies are taken with the task of educating our children, yet home schooling is only one aspect of our lives, there are so many other dynamics. The intensity of home schooling often leaves little time for our own hearts and the journeys of self. And it is not unusual to struggle making the pieces fit together into a unified, healthy, and dynamic whole. Often we are so close to our own situations that we cannot even make heads or tails of what the pieces are, let alone which ones may need tweaking.

It is in these places where I have found another's voice and questions speaking into my own life to be invaluable. For it's always good to dig through the piles of dirty dishes and laundry to find values perhaps forgotten for a time. In coming away with new perspective and insight into my own life I can then lay my realities and our limitations before my God. In this I find His covering and His care. I am refreshed and renewed. It is my heart's desire to have passed this on to you in turn.

I'd like to think we have had a really good conversation and a cup of tea together. I trust you have been encouraged to walk confidently in the choices before you while resting in the limitations that naturally drive and accompany them. Thanks for taking this journey with me through the labyrinths of our hearts and homes. May you go forward with an increasing depth, richness, and direction to your own home schooling.

Appendix
Reproducible Forms

Putting it Together

What the Study is Offering (knowledge to be gained)	What We are Bringing to the Study	Skills We Need to Learn (What skills do I need to train?)	Synopsis of the Purposes and Goals of the Semester

Making an Assessment—**Step One**

Semester's Focus: _____

Supportive Literature	Supportive Resource Books

Paper-Based Brainstorming—**Step Two**

Brainstorming and Detailing

Brainstorming	Detailing					
	Phone & Email	Address	Directions	Hours of Operation	Cost	Misc. Info

Brainstorming & Detailing Form—**Step Two**

Categories	Resources
Literature	
Reference Resources	
Experiments & Crafts	
Bookwork	
Field Trips	
Art/ Artists/ Poetry	
Videos	
Misc.	

Categorizing Resources Form #1—**Step Three**

Categories	Older Resources	Younger Resources
Literature		
Reference Resources		
Experiments & Crafts		
Bookwork		
Field Trips		
Art/Artists & Poetry		
Videos		
Misc.		

Categorizing Resources Form #2—**Step Three**

Blank Months

Sunday	Monday	Tuesday	Wednesday	Thursday	Friday	Saturday

Calendar Blanks—**Step Four**

Topic: _____

Week #	Dates	Sub-Topic

Semester Outline Form—**Step Four**

Week _____

Sub-Topic:_____

Reading	
Worksheets	
Language Study	
Writing Assignments	
Hands-on	
Art/Artists & Poetry	
Field Trip	
Video	
Misc.	
Other	

Weekly Outline Form #1—**Step Five**

Week _____
Sub-Topic:_____

Component	Older	Younger
Reading		
Worksheets		
Language Study		
Writing Assignments		
Hands-on		
Art/Artists & Poetry		
Field Trip/ Video/ Misc.		
Other		

Weekly Outline Form #2—**Step Five**

Week _____
Sub-Topic: _____

Component	Monday	Tuesday	Wednesday	Thursday	Friday
Reading					
Worksheets					
Language Study					
Vocabulary & Spelling					
Writing Assignments					
Hands-on					
Art/Artists & Poetry					
Field Trip/ Video/ Misc.					
Other					

Daily Outline Form #1—**Step Six**

Week _____
Sub-Topic: _____

Component	Monday	Tuesday	Wednesday	Thursday	Friday
Language Study					
Read Aloud					
Worksheet					
Science/ Socials					
Math					
Art					
Hands-on					
Field Trip					
Misc.					
Other					

Daily Outline Form #2—**Step Six**

Resources

Unschooling

Teach Your Own: The John Holt Book of Homeschooling
John Holt
Perseus Publishing, 2003
ISBN 0-7382-0694-6

Wholehearted Education

Educating the WholeHearted Child
Clay and Sally Clarkson
Whole Heart Ministries, 1996
ISBN 1888692006

Independent Learning

The Teenage Liberation Handbook: How to quit school and get a real life and education
Grace Llewellyn
Lowry House Publishers, 1998
ISBN 0-9629591-0-3

Unit Studies

How to Create Your Own Unit Study
Valerie Bendt
Common Sense Press, 1994
ISBN 1880892421

Heart of Wisdom
Robin Sampson
Heart of Wisdom Publishing Inc., 2005
ISBN 0970181671

Konos, Inc.
P.O. Box 250
Anna, TX 75409
972-924-2712 Fax 972-924-2733
info@konos.com
www.konos.com

Classical Education

The Well-Trained Mind: A Guide to Classical Education at Home
S. Wise Bauer, Jessie Wise
W. W. Norton & Company, 2004
ISBN 0393059278

Charlotte Mason

For the Children's Sake: Foundations of Education for Home and School
Susan Schaeffer Macaulay
Crossway Books, 1984
ISBN 089107290X

A Charlotte Mason Companion: Personal Reflections on the Gentle Art of Learning
Karen Andreola
Charlotte Mason Research & Supply, 1998
ISBN 1889209023

Textbook/Workbook

Christian Liberty Academy
www.homeschools.org

A Beka
www.abeka.com

Bob Jones University Press
www.bjupress.com

Sonlight Curriculum
www.sonlight.com

Tree of Life School and Book Service
www.treeoflifeathome.com

Alpha Omega Publications
www.aop.com

Accelerated Christian Education
www.aceministries.com

Christian Light Education
www.clp.org

Books referenced, in order of mention

Drawing for Older Children & Teens
Mona Brookes,
Penguin Putnam Inc., 1991
ISBN 0-87477-661-9

In Their Own Way
Thomas Armstrong
Jeremy P. Tarcher/Putnam (Penguin-Putnam)
ISBN 1-58542-051-4

Hints on Child Training
H. Clay Trumbull
Great Expectations Co., 1993
ISBN 188393401X

Dumbing Us Down
John Taylor Gatto
New Society Publishers, 2002
ISBN 0-86571-448-7

Saxon Math 65: An Incremental Development
Second Edition
Saxon Publishers, 1995

Math-U-See
www.mathusee.com

Spell to Write and Read
Wanda Sanseri
Back Home Industries, 2002
ISBN 1-880045-24-9

The W.I.S.E. Guide for Spelling
Wanda Kennedy Sanseri
Back Home Industries, 2000
ISBN 1-880045-21-4

My Side of the Mountain
Jean Craighead George
Puffin Books
ISBN 0140348107

Swiss Family Robinson
J.D. Wyss
Puffin Books, 1994
ISBN 0-14-036718-7

Considering God's Creation
www.eagleswingsed.com

Encyclopedia of World Geography
Published by Usborne
ISBN 0-7460-4206-X

Arctic & Antarctica
Barbara Taylor
Dorling Kindersley, 1995
ISBN 0-7894-5850-0

The Cranky Blue Crab
Dawn L. Watkins
Bob Jones University Press, 1990
ISBN 0-89084-506-9

The Secret Garden
Frances Hodgson Burnett
Scholastic, 2000
ISBN 0590240773

It Couldn't Just Happen: Faith-Building Evidences for Young People
Lawrence O. Richards
Word Publishing, 1989
ISBN 0-8499-0715-2

Mountains & Valleys
Steve and Jane Parker
Thunder Bay Press, 1996
ISBN 1-57145-026-2

Dance in the Desert
Madeleine L'Engle
Farrar, Straus & Giroux, 1969
ISBN 0374416842

The Deer in the Wood
Laura Ingalls Wilder
HarperTrophy, 1999
ISBN 0-06-443498-2

Where the River Begins
Thomas Locker
Puffin Pied Piper Books, 1984
ISBN 0-14-054595-6

Antarctica: Journey to the Pole
Peter Lerangis
Published by Scholastic Inc., 2000
ISBN 0-439-16387-0

Illustrated Thesaurus
Jane Bingham & Fiona Chandler
Usborne Publishing Company, 2001
ISBN 0746046111

Nature Crafts for Kids
Gwen Diehn & Terry Krautwurst
Sterling Publishing Company, 1992
ISBN 0-8069-8372-8

Science Crafts for Kids
Gwen Diehn & Terry Krautwurst
Sterling Publishing Company, 1994
ISBN 0-8069-0283-3

How Science Works
Judith Hahn
Readers Digest, 1991
ISBN 0-89577-382-1

How Weather Works
Michael Allaby
Readers Digest, 1995
ISBN 0-89577-612-X

What Shall I Draw?
Ray Gibson
Usborne Publishing, 1995
ISBN 0-7460-2024-4

Drawing with Children
Mona Brookes
G.P. Putnam's Sons, 1996
ISBN 0-87477-827-1

The Art of Robert Bateman
Robert Bateman
Madison Press Books, 1988
ISBN -0-670-82639-1

Great Wildlife Search
1994 Usborne Publishing
ISBN 07460 3332X

The Usborne Complete First Book of Nature
Usborne Publishing Ltd., 1990
ISBN 0-74600563-6

The Wildlife Year
Readers Digest Association, 1993
ISBN 0276420128

When I was Young in the Mountains
Cynthia Rylant
Puffin, 1985
ISBN 978-0525441984

Famous Explorers
Daniel Rogers
Hove: Wayland, 1993
ISBN 0750206705

The Yearling
Marjorie Kinnan Rawlings
Aladdin Paperbacks, 2001
ISBN 0-689-84623-1

A House for Hermit Crab
Eric Carle
Scholastic, 1987
ISBN 0-590-42567-6

Lost in the Fog
Irving Bacheller; adapted and illustrated by Loretta Krupinski
Little, Brown & Company, 1990
ISBN 0-316-07462-4

How Nature Works
David Burnie
Dorling Kindersley
Readers Digest, 1991
ISBN 0-89577-391-0

Excellence in Writing
www.writing-edu.com

Swallows and Amazons
Arthur Ransome
Originally published by Jonathan Cape, 1930
ISBN 0-224-60631-X

GIVING MY LIFE TO CHRIST

from Cyndy Lavoie

We all live with sin. In the Bible we are told, "For all have sinned and fall short of the glory of God" (Rom. 3:23). I don't have to think too hard to recognize this within myself.

We are told that the penalty of sin is death. "For the wages of sin is death" (Rom. 6:23).

We are also told that Jesus Christ came to shed his blood that we may have life. "But God shows his love for us in that while we were still sinners, Christ died for us" (Rom. 5:8).

This is His gift to us. "For by grace you have been saved through faith. And this is not your own doing; it is the gift of God, not a result of works, so that no one may boast" (Eph. 2:8-9).

I accepted Christ into my heart as a little girl, saying, "Jesus, would You come into my heart and take away my sin? I want to live with You forever. Amen." Romans 10:13 says:

"Everyone who calls on the name of the Lord will be saved."

At that young age I didn't realize that I was inviting him into my life in a very general way. It was a very good beginning, to be sure, but only a beginning nonetheless. At that time the Holy Spirit put a seal upon my spirit, marking me His own. And in that seal I continued through life, always with a sense of Him encompassing me.

It was not until I was much older, my middle 30s to be exact, that I began to learn the value of inviting Christ into the individual rooms of my heart. For by the time I had accepted Christ as a 6-year-old child, I already had places in my heart—rooms, so to speak—that were closed off and with the key thrown away. Each room represented a decision or commitment my heart had made in my formative years. They included pride, fear, shame, and commitments to self-sufficiency, to name but a few.

Some very difficult challenges began to reveal my heart for what it was, and the inadequacy of my self-sufficiency. When Christ asked, "So, Cyndy, how is that self-sufficiency working for you?" my only reply was, "Not so good, thanks." And ever so gently and patiently He began to ask if I would be willing to open the rooms of my heart to Him, to allow Him into those dark places of shame, pride, and fear. It was as the Bible says: "Behold, you delight in truth in the inward being, and you teach me wisdom in the secret heart" (Psalm 51:6).

I was terrified, but what did I have to lose? And so I began to invite Him once more, this time in very specific ways. "Jesus, I confess to you my sin of self-sufficiency. I see how it has kept me from Your sufficiency. So today, in the name of the Lord Jesus Christ, I renounce a spirit of self-sufficiency in my life, and the judgment that I had to care for myself because You weren't good enough for the job. I cancel the assignments and curses of the enemy who, due to my sin, has had authority to wreak havoc in my life in this area. I invite you, Jesus, to be my self-sufficiency, and I commit to trusting You and not myself.

Would you make this place new in me?"

I cannot begin to tell you the beauty, simplicity, and yet power of a prayer like this.

Christ died that we may have life, and it is through His name that life becomes our own. It is because of the blood of Christ that my sin, my dead places, can be made new and have life. As I invited Christ into these rooms, my heart began to live as never before. Ezekiel 11:19 says: "I will give them an undivided heart and put a new spirit in them; I will remove the heart of stone from their flesh and give them a heart of flesh."

So profoundly different yet similar, I also learned that the sins committed against me are covered by Christ's blood sacrifice as well. This means that I do not have to live under the effects of harms done to me. The cost of keeping these events to myself and carrying them myself is just another form of pride and self-sufficiency. It is an "I can take care of this myself, thank you very much" kind of attitude. But in this I miss out on so much. I miss out on a real, vibrant, life offered by our living Lord Jesus Christ.

And so I began to invite Him into my "harms," which are those places within my soul that feel dead, that leave me wondering if I am irreversibly messed up, places where I barely even know that I am missing out on life. "Jesus, there is this black, ugly place in my soul," I was able to pray. "Do you know what he/she did to me?" "Jesus, that was really awful. I think I might even hate the person who did that." "But Jesus, today I stand in the blood covering of the Lord Jesus Christ and I extend forgiveness to _____. I put my faith in You, Jesus, that You will deal with that person as you see fit. I accept your "salvation" of my dark places, and I relinquish to You my hatreds and bitterness, my fears and shames, and I accept Your life in the name of the Lord Jesus Christ."

I share this because in the midst of home schooling we come face to face with our own deficiencies a lot of the time. Home schooling has many beautiful moments; I have found it is also pretty messy. Perhaps that is because into my home schooling I bring inner decisions made in childhood that stand against God's ways, despite my verbal assents to His leadership. And I bring into my home schooling the effects of the harms done against me, and my own subconscious—or even conscious—hateful and bitter decisions, decisions that stand against the Savior.

Because home schooling can bring us face to face with our own black places, it is a wonderful venue by which to see, quite clearly and consistently, where the Savior is *not* in residence. And once I see these places, I can begin to invite Him, specifically, into places I may have never invited Him before.

In Revelations 3:20 Jesus says, "Behold, I stand at the door and knock. If anyone hears my voice and opens the door, I will come in to him and eat with him, and he with me." This beautiful verse speaks of fellowship. The Hebrews would not eat with an enemy. Eating with someone declared that person to be a friend. I have experienced this eating with Jesus. I have experienced the delight of opening my darkness and death to Him and the very life He came to give. It is as I open my dark places to Him that His light illuminates and makes new what was once given over to death. And I am slowly made a new creature. I am no longer irreversibly messed up.

As I continue to parent, I know that Jesus is there for my children as well, that in His time He will make Himself known to them also as Savior—a Savior not just in terms of getting to heaven, but a Savior for their todays and their tomorrows, for their sins and their "harms."

And so I pray covering over them. "God I lift _____ before You. I commit _____ into Your care and keeping, and I stand in the name of the Lord Jesus Christ declaring a covering of His saving blood over _____ vulnerabilities. I stand against all curses and assignments of the enemy which would seek to take advantage of their vulnerabilities, and I pray Your salvation over them this day, for Your glory and honor."

The thing is that unless Christ shows up in very real and tangible ways, we are toast. Life is just too messy, and we are just too imperfect. I too am imperfect. And so I invite Him, day after day, "God, come into our day today. God, come into my darkness. God, show up amid our messes. God, I invite Your specific salvation of me and mine this day."

And, as it says in Jeremiah 29:12-13, He honors this. "Then you will call upon me and come and pray to me, and I will hear you. You will seek me and find me. When you seek me with all your heart … ."

I encourage you to keep on seeking Him in the midst of your lives. May He be your Savior in new and fresh ways every day as you invite Him. As it says in Psalm 69:13:

"But as for me, my prayer is to you, O Lord. At an acceptable time, O God, in the abundance of your steadfast love answer me in your saving faithfulness."

With Blessings,
Cyndy Lavoie

CrossHouse

P.O. Box 461592   1-877-212-3022(Office)

Garland, TX 75046   1-888-252-3022 (Fax)

ORDER MORE COPIES OF
Home Education By Design
BY PHONE, FAX, or MAIL

Date:

Bill to:

Phone:

Signature:

Order#:

Ship to:

Card #

Exp. date:

Item	Quantity	Price	Total
Home Education by Design		$12.95	
Sales Tax (8.25%) Texas Residents Only			
Shipping ($3.00 for first book, 50 cents for each addtl.)			
Grand Total			

Printed in the United States
76955LV00006B/3-212

9 780929 292496